BOLD COURAGE

HOW OWNING YOUR AWESOME CHANGES EVERYTHING

PAULA MORAND

Published by Motivational Press, Inc.
1777 Aurora Road
Melbourne, Florida, 32935
www.MotivationalPress.com

Copyright 2016 © by Paula Morand

All Rights Reserved

No part of this book may be reproduced or transmitted in any form by any means: graphic, electronic, or mechanical, including photocopying, recording, taping or by any information storage or retrieval system without permission, in writing, from the authors, except for the inclusion of brief quotations in a review, article, book, or academic paper. The authors and publisher of this book and the associated materials have used their best efforts in preparing this material. The authors and publisher make no representations or warranties with respect to accuracy, applicability, fitness or completeness of the contents of this material. They disclaim any warranties expressed or implied, merchantability, or fitness for any particular purpose. The authors and publisher shall in no event be held liable for any loss or other damages, including but not limited to special, incidental, consequential, or other damages. If you have any questions or concerns, the advice of a competent professional should be sought.

Manufactured in the United States of America.

ISBN: 978-1-62865-327-4

CONTENTS

FOREWORD BY JUSTIN SACHS 6
ABOUT THE AUTHOR 8
INTRODUCTION 9

PART 1   **SERIOUSLY, HOW DID I END UP HERE?** **11**
CHAPTER 1   WHEN PUSH COMES TO SHOVE 11
CHAPTER 2   WHEN INSPIRATION STRIKES 22
CHAPTER 3   THE REALITY PARADIGM 29
CHAPTER 4   THE PACE YOU TRAVEL 37
CHAPTER 5   THE CASE FOR BOLD COURAGE 47

PART 2   **THE SEARCH FOR SIGNIFICANCE** **54**
CHAPTER 6   A WORLD OF RELEVANCE 54
CHAPTER 7   THE WILLINGNESS EFFECT 61
CHAPTER 8   TRUST THE PROCESS 68
CHAPTER 9   BE UNCOMFORTABLE: BE BOLD WHERE YOU NEED TO BE ..74

PART 3   **A CASE CALLED WORTHY** **82**
CHAPTER 10   FREEDOM THROUGH FAILING 82
CHAPTER 11   EMBRACING CHAOS 88
CHAPTER 12   WHEN THE STAKES GET HIGH 96
CHAPTER 13   JUST ONE THING 103
CHAPTER 14   SECRET TO BEING A GAME CHANGER 110

PART 4   **THE QUEST FOR SUCCESS** **117**
CHAPTER 15   YOUR STORY MEANS SOMETHING 117
CHAPTER 16   PERFECTLY FLAWED 123
CHAPTER 17   THE ART OF GIVING 130

PART 5	**LEADING THE SHIFT** **137**
CHAPTER 18	EMPOWERMENT THROUGH FEEDBACK 137
CHAPTER 19	PREPARING TO LAUNCH 145
CHAPTER 20	THE ART OF WINNING 153
CHAPTER 21	RELATIONSHIPS MATTER 160

PART 6	**PUTTING IT ALL TOGETHER** **166**
CHAPTER 22	CONNECTING THE DOTS................................166
CHAPTER 23	THE SUCCESS TRACKER SYSTEM 172
CHAPTER 24	LET FAITH BE YOUR SHELTER 186

"This book is dedicated to my amazing team who made it possible to bring a vision to life. Words cannot express my appreciation, especially, for the devotion of Victoria Craig who saw the potential for greatness and helped bring it to fruition."

FOREWORD

BY JUSTIN SACHS

Packing your bags and heading out on a journey to the unknown is always interesting and a little bit frightening.

So let me be the first to congratulate you on your decision to go out of your comfort zone this year and head down the highway of experiences to find your awesome.

The first step is always the hardest, and you have my respect for taking it.

But you won't have to travel alone. In this book we'll provide you with innovative steps and a rich toolkit full of all kinds of great stories and strategies to help you stay on track and reach your destination.

In this book the voice of the narrative is that of Paula Morand, an accomplished businesswoman and motivational speaker. Her encounter with the darkest side of tragedy as a young woman first introduced her to the counter-balance of courage.

The concept of *"Bold Courage"* stayed with her as the years passed and she developed her mentoring skills. Now it has come alive in a book that reminds all of us we can make changes in our life journey, no matter how many detours we are directed into by circumstances or how many times our choices get us lost.

You can use this book to get really creative about your personal and career development. It's full of new and innovative tools that will take you on a journey of growth. For example, who knew that a personal experience time capsule could bring clarity to the present?

I encourage you to stay on course as you make your journey. It is easy to pack up your intentions and head out, only to get sidetracked the second day of the road.

Instead, give yourself time to read and enjoy the explorations of your journey. There's no harm in having some time and gaining some insight along the way.

Remember old stories, gather new experiences and let them morph into this elusive charm that is an awesome life!

To your interesting journey,

Justin Sachs
*International Best Selling Author of **The Power of Persistence**
and 10 other business and leadership books.*

ABOUT THE AUTHOR

Paula Morand is a leadership building, revenue boosting, strategy expanding keynote speaker, author and visionary. This dreaming big and being bold expert brings her vibrant energy, humor and wisdom to ignite individuals, organizations and communities to lead change, growth and impact in a more bold fashion. 23 years, 25,000 clients, 19 countries, 11 books, Former radio personality, 10x award winning entrepreneur, humorous emcee and acknowledged as one of the country's top influencers.

One of her favorite pieces of advice to those seeking to take control of their lives is to "dream big, be bold and own your awesome."

She is the founder and visionary behind Paula Morand Enterprises which includes a premiere leadership and training institute that has served more than 25,000 clients and a global outreach foundation.

Her newest program, **Dream Big and Be Bold,** which is a foundation for her newest book, is set to reach an even larger scale.

INTRODUCTION

Dear Reader,

If you are like most people existing in this age of distraction, you start each Monday morning with your stomach in knots, your to-do-list long enough to paper a wall, and your sense of disengagement between the life you live and the life you want growing rapidly.

Your work no longer gives you a strong sense of purpose and your ship of dreams is moving further out into stormy seas. You fear it may never come back.

I have good news for you.

You don't have to keep living like that.

You still have lots of time and energy to become a game changer in your own life. You just can't see it from the crowded, noisy, goal-obstructed viewpoint you have on life right now.

All you need is *Bold Courage to dream big and be bold* and some simple tools and you can find your own awesome again.

This book, my eleventh, is all about shifting your perspective, discovering your possibilities, making the decision to take risks, and learning to play a bigger game of life.

I started my first company at the end of 26 in the most dire of circumstances a person could find themselves in. Four years later I sold it and spent the next 20 years investing in building companies that increased human potential through consulting, coaching and training.

I know what it feels like to go from a life of desperation to a life of purpose. I can take you on that journey so you will arrive at a new place of personal freedom and growth unlike anything you may imagine.

You will learn many things in this book such as:

» How to identify your breaking point

- » How to let go and create a new starting point in life
- » How to prepare your warrior mindset
- » How to give yourself permission to release your mental shackles
- » How to believe in yourself again
- » How to stop the noise and find your purpose in the clarity of silence
- » How to embrace your vulnerability as a treasure to be shared with your community

Most of all, I will guide you on a journey to create lasting changes in your life.

You will learn how to find and keep inspiration as a smart life and work strategy. You will open your door wide open to happiness and satisfaction without abandoning who you are.

My words ring authentically through each page because, as you will learn from my stories, I am writing about what I know best. I am weaving through these words the innovative solutions that evolved from the fabric of my own life when I felt despair.

You will see that no matter how successful you become in the eyes of others, you may still be plagued by doubts and insecurities. That is normal and ordinary.

What is extraordinary is when you can corral your self-doubts and find space to grow your dreams and expand to the larger life you are meant to live.

I hope you will join me on this exciting journey. If we can move with *Bold Courage* together, we will both reach our destination faster.

Yours with faith in you,
Paula

PART 1

SERIOUSLY, HOW DID I END UP HERE?

CHAPTER 1

WHEN PUSH COMES TO SHOVE

We all have a breaking point.

For me, it happened during one of the most challenging business projects I have ever undertaken in my professional and entrepreneurial journey.

For eighteen years I built a satisfying career as a successful business and leadership coach. I was fortunate enough to work with amazing organizations and individuals helping them manage and create strategies and new ideas for positive change and growth. Innovation and creativity are in my blood and these quickly became a differentiator in how I conducted and delivered business through my company. It's what gets me excited and really charged up, so it was a logical decision to move my company vision to the next level of innovation.

The next four years were a whirlwind, while our team worked on a technology project that measured real time productivity and satisfaction. We created an analytic software and leadership solution to help organizational leaders coach and manage employee engagement while fostering leadership excellence. We linked it to improving corporate culture and bottom line results, which is what made it so magical.

It was all consuming, but we loved it. It took a tremendous number of hours, and even at that we squeezed out more. We travelled constantly from one end of the continent to the other to share our early stage successes and growth in an attempt to entice new clients and further investment. It became even more exhilarating when we made breakthroughs in our research and development process. The project clearly had the possibility of a huge financial return. We saw it and so did our early investors.

During our fourth year, the pressure increased. We launched a new investment round, working on raising an additional $1.5 million in financing. From Boston, to Toronto, to New York, we met with technology-focused investors. The juggle between financing the business, building the technology, and acquiring new customers made this a constant dance of setting the right priorities.

On one particular trip to New York City, I was invited to pitch my company to a room full of investors at one of the statelier and impressive law offices in Lower Manhattan. There were 27 people around a massive boardroom table and I had about 30 minutes to pitch my business case, answer questions and entice investors to come onboard.

The pitch was on short notice, but in true entrepreneurial spirit, I accepted the challenge. It was high stakes and needless to say I was a little rattled. I pitched my business case for 10 minutes and was peppered with questions for the next 20.

Things didn't go exactly as I had hoped. The potential investors not only didn't understand the human resources industry sector that we were selling to, but they had no interest in the $500 billion dollar problem we were solving. What they did have were big egos and a keen interest in demonstrating how inept they thought the idea and its presenter were. I did not get any investors that day.

Even though I had given hundreds of pitches in the past, somehow in this particular setting, I felt beaten up. One woman in the group was so embarrassed by the behavior of her colleagues that she followed me outside to apologize for them. She was sweet, but her words had little effect on me. The damage to my confidence was done. I had just spent $5,000 to be there and the money was flushed away along with a part of my self-worth. At that moment, the energy and hope of the previous four years was replaced with anger, frustration and disappointment.

This was one of those moments that felt like the perfect storm. Have you experienced those moments? You know you were prepared for the situation, you had rehearsed it mentally, but then everything fell into chaos and confusion. It is like watching a movie where you know what is about to happen, you can see it coming, but you can't do anything to stop it.

I left the building and walked up Park Avenue alone with my self-confidence replaced with self-loathing and remorse.

I'd just hit my breaking point. For good and bad, I had some tough decisions to make.

CHANGES AHEAD

For me, that decision point precipitated a season of change.

Managing change after an emotional crash can take you on a journey from excitement and positive expectation to fear, uncertainty, and dread. When your confidence is fractured, decisions don't come easily. Even though I was ready for change and I was in the proper mindset, I still found myself second guessing my choices.

When I first looked back, I perceived this experience as the starting point for one of the largest failures of my career. That was true in some respects because it eventually led to the demise of our multimillion dollar project.

But all life experiences give birth to wisdom if you let them.

Upon further reflection of this experience, I accepted it as a gift. I emerged with new knowledge and experience. This is a gift that I am now able to share with you.

Most importantly, it was the day I found my bold courage and started my journey to "awesome."

The story isn't over yet. All I know for sure is that beauty is born in the darkness of a storm.

You may also reach your breaking point when you fall into despair. You lose hope for what could have been and see only what isn't happening in your life. You feel life is out of your control and you can't pull it together or "manage" your way through it.

In your breaking point, your mind becomes foggy and your world feels like it is going so fast, but you are moving in slow motion. It is increasingly difficult to make decisions and you constantly second-guess yourself. You are smothered in self-doubt, blame and failure.

Your emotions are on high alert and even though you may not think you are showing signs of stress, the sleepless nights soon get the best of you. Your response to managing life becomes reactive versus proactive, often giving way to more rattled emotions instead of rational thinking.

To top things off, your physical health declines and your mental state continues in this place of fragility and uncertainty. At this point, you start to move into numbness and feel completely powerless as you enter a state of being completely overwhelmed. Does any of this sound familiar?

Somewhere in the midst of my breaking point, I realized that I had to stop the fall. I had enough of negative behaviors, bad patterns and personal triggers.

IDENTIFYING TRIGGER POINTS

Triggers are people or situations that cause you to react negatively either psychologically or physically or both.

Here is an example of one of my personal triggers and its resulting negative behaviors: When I was a child I learned that watching out for others and going out of my way to please them was the right thing to do. I came to this conclusion based on my own interpretation of my parent's rule to respect my elders.

When I felt someone older than me was judging me, chaos and internal upset happened. Being judged by someone older than me was my trigger. My pattern was instant belief that I was not working hard enough and was falling short of my skills and abilities.

The negative behavior that resulted from this trigger and pattern was for me to try harder at all costs. I wanted to be noticed and validated for my effort and my "good" work by those elders. The damage to myself in the process of improving my efforts was penance for not getting the particular task right the first time. I know now that this situation was created entirely by me. Nobody ever asked me to do better at all costs, without any regard to myself.

I certainly did find attention in being known for things like the hardest worker, the smartest girl, the politest and the sweetest, for example. What people didn't know was the damage I was doing to myself by putting everyone else first and allowing them to dictate my worthiness.

You have your own trigger points, patterns and behaviors that happen as a result of living. It is completely normal.

Trigger points can also be positive. I am a highly competitive person and when put in a competitive environment I will excel at my task. The trigger is the competition, the pattern is excitement and the desire to be the best, and the behavior is hard work and excellent results. This is an excellent trait and not something I wish to dismiss.

The triggers, patterns and behaviors I want to get rid of are those negative ones that do nothing except tear down my confidence and make me feel inferior. If I didn't do something to break the cycle of my triggers, patterns and behaviors that weren't serving me in a healthy way, nothing would change.

I had to face those triggers and let them go or I would remain in a place of frustration, disappointment, anger and even rage.

Trigger points are sneaky disrupters that lie in wait deep within all of us. In a state of uncertainty, there is no telling when they will bubble up. Sometimes they spill over in tears and sometimes they erupt like a volcano.

That is the moment I chose to stop the decline and start living my life with more intention.

THE DECISION TO LET GO

I had enough of all those things that contributed to my sense of hopelessness and failure. It was time to make decisions and change my circumstances. If my situation was to change, I had the ability and freedom to make it happen. Now I know that you do too.

To combat stress overload I started asking myself some questions. What if I focused on being more proactive in my life and developed a stronger sense of self? I could insulate myself with self-talk that triggered new behaviors, mindsets and actions for a more positive outlook. What if I changed my storyline and moved myself out of this negative holding pattern? My spirit was screaming a resounding yes!

It is not easy to let go. We are our own worst enemy when it comes to holding on to things that no longer serve us. We cling to old resentments, limiting beliefs, and ill-conceived assumptions, all of which cause us grief as we age. We use our past hurts, disappointments, judgments and regrets as excuses for not living our ideal life.

> "My experience has helped me to understand that we must all learn to let go before we reach our breaking points.

My experience has helped me to understand that we must all learn to let go before we reach our breaking points.

Letting go is a key component to embracing "bold courage." Letting go is your biggest opportunity for growth and change.

When you change the dialogue from "I can't" to "I could" you set the stage for a new starting pointing life.

From that starting point, you will be able to recognize your situation and how you feel about it.

How do you ignite this process of self-change? You begin by digging deep and recognizing how and why you got to the place you are in. You take ownership of the role that you played in getting there. You let go of those bad things like missed opportunities, failures and unwise decisions. You stop repeatedly blaming yourself for them.

> Letting go is your biggest opportunity for growth and change

It takes a lot of courage to get real with yourself but when you're willing to do it, growth happens. Through this growth you then have the opportunity to re-evaluate what you want and don't want in your life.

That's exactly what I did. Now I realize that learning to let go gave me new freedom and confidence. My resiliency was born and I found renewed life where my creativity and innovation could flourish.

DREAMS UNFULFILLED

By the time you are in your late teens, you have a picture of what you believe a fulfilled life looks like for you. This picture becomes the driving force for making decisions in your adult years. It often includes your ideas about when you will be married, when you will have a family, where you will travel, and what your career will be. All of these dreams start to anchor an expectation of what your ideal life will be.

It's when that dream doesn't go exactly as planned that the art of letting go plays an important role. The fact is, everyone wants to live the dream, but the truth is that life rarely goes as planned. If that has happened to you, the good news is that you are not alone. Everyone has a story of a dream unfulfilled. Fortunately we all have the power to decide to let go of certain dreams or reframe them. We can also take control of dreams we want to keep, but which have not yet happened.

I had to learn to do both. I took control of those things that made sense and released the rest. A key thing I had to let go of was fear for my future and shame from my past. I needed to take control of the present day.

To do that I embraced bold courage and prepared my mindset like a warrior ready to move into battle. I knew that to be successful I needed to be committed to my journey, focused on it and more intentional about what I wanted to happen. I wanted more positivity in my life and had to focus on that to move forward. This shift made a huge impact and created lasting change for me.

REFRAMING THE EXPERIENCE

The journey to becoming more intentional in life starts with reframing your bad experiences. For example, I reframed my experience of travelling to New York City with a 24-hour turnaround and subsequently coming away with no investment. My spirit could have been crushed for the rest of my life and I could have become professionally debilitated. But I wanted my life to be different. That's not how I wanted the story to end.

I made the choice not to focus on the frustration and upset of the trip. Instead I reframed it as a valuable life lesson. I delivered a clear, concise pitch and offered an investment opportunity that was world class, and I learned that not everyone loved this idea. Once I saw it as a lesson, it gave me a chance to change things. That day I took a piece of my life back, a piece that I had allowed to be robbed. As odd as it may sound now, I'm thankful for those rude investors.

I now realize that this experience was one of the greatest gifts that I have ever been given on so many levels. Honestly, there is something cathartic about choosing wisdom over failure. There are lessons to be learned from past experiences. There is no honor or value in being bound by the decisions and actions you have already experienced and cannot change. What's done is done and all you can do is live right now. Grant yourself permission to release those things that are holding you back and open the door to new possibilities.

I recognized that if I didn't do something to break the cycle of my triggers, patterns, and behaviors that weren't serving me; they would continue to keep me in a place of frustration, disappointment, anger and rage. Instead I chose to let go and own my awesome. Thus began the journey of finding my way back to me again.

It is a journey you can take as well. You can let go of your frustrations, disappointments and unfulfilled dreams and find your own awesome. I invite you to join me on this journey to finding your way back to your authentic self. This day and this book can be your starting point to find the bold courage to take back your life and live it on your terms.

One of the sources of wisdom for our personal journeys comes to me from a Japanese tradition that has always fascinated me.

They have perfected the art of Kintsugi, or fixing pottery in need of repair. This is the process of mending broken objects by filling the cracks with gold. They believe the breakage and repair process is part of the rich history of an object. What I find intriguing about this tradition is there is no attempt to hide the damage. Instead it is highlighted and the object becomes more priceless than it was in its original perfect condition.

Our lives can be honored in the same fashion. Our stories mean something. They are what make our lives unique, authentic, and intriguing. Our stories help to inspire and remind us that life is both rich and fragile.

It is through our willingness to illuminate our flaws, failures and imperfections that confidence and acceptance returns.

CHAPTER 1

The bestselling author Malcolm Gladwell, in his book *The Outliers, The Story of Success* (Little, Brown & Company 2008) made popular the idea known as "the 10,000 Hour Rule." In examining the factors that contribute to high degrees of success, he theorized that the key to achieving world class success in any skill is primarily a matter of practicing it correctly for a total of 10,000 hours.

Learning to let go is a tremendous and useful skill, and you must practice it like any other to become good at it.

The same can be said for learning to be mindful and intentional about living in the present.

As you progress through your own journey, realize that creating positive change takes time, commitment and courage. It is, however, the best investment you will make in this life.

The process of learning to let go allows you to build a new discipline for managing fear. It allows you to choose wisdom over fear and see your situation in a new way. That is the way new decisions and future successes will be measured, not with a yardstick from the past.

For me, the wisdom I gained from reaching my breaking point was the exact catalyst I needed to launch into an exciting new era of my life.

You can do that too. Join me and let's get started.

A STORY OF HANNAH

I've worked with thousands of people throughout the years, but one client stands out in my memory. She was a professional career woman who had hired me as her executive coach to help her move through a period of overwhelming responsibility and high stress.

When I first met her, I sensed her entire being was filled with deep self-limiting beliefs of not being good enough and not deserving enough, despite her professional success. Somewhere from her past, she believed the idea that she was not worthy of greatness.

Instead of owning what was awesome about herself, she operated within a mindset of failure. Internal messages of self-loathing were toxic and draining for this talented woman and it was damaging her professional success as well as her personal relationships. She stopped seeing her own potential and I could see she was at a stalemate in her career and her life path.

She may not have been at her final breaking point, but she was close and certainly needed help. She had endured enough, wanted change and by hiring me, she was showing readiness to start the process of letting go.

But all of us like the security that comes from long-held ideas about the way things are and how we are supposed to live our lives. Letting go is never easy for any of us, and it wasn't easy for Hannah.

It took bold courage for her to realize that most of her roadblocks were self-imposed. She faced the reality that she was self-sabotaging her own success. Her triggers, patterns and behaviors had become debilitating.

Through our time together she was able to recognize that and start to shift the negative patterns into a more positive approach. Once she did that, she was able to make better decisions and choices for herself.

PART 1

SERIOUSLY, HOW DID I END UP HERE?

CHAPTER 2

WHEN INSPIRATION STRIKES

Sunlight. There is nothing more beautiful and inspiring than the dawn of a brilliant sunrise or the soul-stirring of a gorgeous sunset. I notice the opening and closing of my days more keenly now in the mental place from which I launched the start of the journey to owning my awesome again.

When I am in this place, I feel so good and I look forward to my future. I start asking myself, "What else is possible?" There is a fundamental shift that happens when we consciously change. Instead of being reactive and wondering where to turn next, I force myself to shift my thinking in preparation for the arrival of new opportunities that appear when least expected.

ONE FINE DAY

Watching a sunrise one day, it dawned on me that I had forgotten how to just be me instead of pushing the persona I thought I should be. That realization alone was freeing, yet humbling at the same time. Through that realization I was able to step into my true self, releasing unrealistic expectations and some hang-ups that had been weighing me down for so long.

I rediscovered the roots of who I am and refined those values that are at the core of what is important to me. It reminded me that when I live in direct conflict to what my values are telling me, I will always find myself fighting because the internal and external parts of me will never fully sync.

To own my awesome I had to be willing step to outside of my comfort zone to seek possibilities and learn to wait. There is power in learning to be still as there is wisdom that comes from reflection. That sunrise moment was a perfect place to start infusing more inspiration in my life.

From that day forward, I took action and started feeding my senses with positive, life affirming and feel-good choices in music, food, movies, books, people, activities, experiences and even my choice of words.

I pressed myself to commit to an ongoing daily ritual of speaking, thinking and writing from a place of positivity. This was difficult, especially coming out of a low point. But I knew it was a necessary discipline that would make a huge difference in my life and it did. That simple strategy quickly started pulling me out of my funk, and also gave me a new season of hope and a readiness to take action.

Like many, I crave momentum. Carving new dreams and giving them fresh energy always makes me feel confident and wonderful. I liken that momentum to the feeling when the wind blows through my hair as I stand looking over the ocean with a sea of ideas before me. I feel still, yet I am exhilarated.

My drive for success and impact is sustained from this idea of continually being inspired. Inspiration is what always helps me to only focus on my present or future goals and not fall into the trap of reliving the past. It gives me confidence to make decisions that are aligned with those insatiable dreams that get me out of bed in the morning and awaken me in the middle of the night. It has always been the catalyst for helping me achieve clarity of vision and to refine my focus of what could come next.

COURSE CORRECTION

I had the privilege of travelling to many different countries for my career as a professional speaker consulting on topics of business strategy and leadership. However, I learned there is one other theme that must be present in all of my presentations and that is inspiration. Every individual and organization needs inspiration to drive their motivation and actions towards their desired improvements regardless of their nationality, status or their basic demographics.

I've found that by making sure that there are plenty of inspiring moments and lessons in my material, it is easier to achieve successful outcomes for the audience. By continually driving motivation and action to the audience, it propels them to refine and fine tune positive behaviors that serve them well.

Getting inspired not only opens the doors to new possibilities, but also allows for a change in perspective on life in general. The right perspective can move mountains but the wrong one is the killer of dreams.

It is very important to consider what your point of view is and to question yourself about it. You'll never go wrong by considering if there is a different way to look at a situation or a problem you are trying to solve. That is what perspective is all about. It is a willingness to shift our thoughts in order to see the possibilities from a different and often better solution that makes sense.

If you are willing to shift your perspective, you will often find a better solution to your situation or problem.

I choose to view my life as one that is full of infinite possibilities, choices and opportunities waiting for me to discover. It wasn't always this way for me. The truth is, life can be challenging at times and I have certainly had my share of challenges thus far. To combat those times, I have learned that the art of cultivating curiosity is my best defense.

THE CHASE

When was the last time you had a great idea? I mean the kind of idea that gets you so excited that you know without a doubt you will do anything to see it come to fruition. When was the last time you became so inspired by an idea that you couldn't wait to get out of bed? When was the last time your inspiration was so strong that you couldn't wait to turn your dream into reality? In a perfect world, this would be an easy question to answer. In reality this may not be the case as ideas are plentiful and cheap, but taking action to make them come alive can be a challenge and requires many actions and decisions along the way.

There is value in the constant pursuit of finding and keeping inspiration as a smart life and work strategy. It forces you to stay in the present. It sets the stage for living in a more intentional, focused and inspired way. Creativity allows you to dream, think of ideas, and innovate ways to evolve and grow. To me, that is a plan for increasing and sustaining long term motivation that makes sense.

INSPIRING BUSINESS

The journey to owning your awesome is often met with the task of reflecting on those things that you consider your strengths. One of the best natural gifts I possess is the ability to come up with new, refreshing ideas and different ways to solve problems. It's easy for me to connect solutions to problems with numerous suggestions and ideas in a variety of scenarios and industry sectors. Quite honestly, I thrive off of the process of ideation and brainstorming and built a business doing just that.

Brainstorming and ideation both help unlock new thinking for old subjects and create new opportunities for ideas not ever thought of before. It is the incubation process of new ideas to lead vision about the future. For me, that not only includes the generation of new ideas but also offers a strategic approach to seeing possible solutions from a variety of different lenses. The value in this process, when structured properly, is that it brings about new insights, decisions and provides options when developing a smart plan to manage change, growth and impact in work or life.

I always assumed that everyone had this skill set. It wasn't until I got much older and further into business strategy and consulting that I realized this is not the case. Once I realized my strength, I deliberately worked hard to further hone this skill over the years as I have since learned it is one of the things that makes me awesome.

I draw inspiration from everywhere, as it is a significant part of my plan to help further develop my ideation capabilities for both my clients and myself. It has allowed for new opportunities, collaborations and exciting projects for everyone along the way. Issues are more easily solved and my mind is more open to seeing various ways of achieving the goal.

Ideation and brainstorming also allowed for better client results as it challenged and stretched their thinking (and mine) and has proven to be an important exercise to finding winning solutions. It has helped my clients discover and own their awesome and get inspired to implement a boldness strategy to take them to the next level.

It is amazing what happens when you are inspired, as it always gives a fresh infusion of confidence and hope and you can always use more of that.

Allow yourself to ideate and continually grow and step into a new level of maturity. As an executive coach, one of the trends I have seen over the last 23 years is that individuals and organizations are trying to stay where they are, because maturing means change. To most, managing change in an already chaotic and busy world is just one more thing to burden them.

I understand the hesitation for many to resist change. However, there is a something incredibly gratifying about landing on a sensational new idea and bringing it to life. It could be a personal life change, a new product or service offering, intriguing ad campaign or finding creative ways to connect with a new client.

This is also a great way to be inspired to join a cause, build community or further your career. Being interested in things outside of yourself and being a part of finding new solutions helps mature your thinking and gives you the bold courage to try new things.

INSPIRATION IS A FUEL

It is important to get a clear picture of why inspiration is important to the journey to owning your awesome. Imagine bold courage as the vehicle and inspiration as the fuel to that coveted destination of finding your awesome. As with all vehicles, you will only be able to move it a certain distance before it needs refueling. This makes inspiration a priority.

The road to owning your awesome may be a long journey, so it is vital to make sure that you are consistently fueled with the right inspiration that powers your thinking to keep moving forward in the right direction.

Inspiration is the fuel that supports times when perseverance and resilience are needed to allow us to face adversity, ill health, misfortune, failure and loss, with a knowing that there is hope on the other side. It is through inspiration that we discover our potential for strength, wisdom and endurance.

> Imagine bold courage as the vehicle and inspiration as the fuel to that coveted destination of finding your awesome.

USE INSPIRATION

I have learned to take simple ideas, give them focus and put them into action for successful outcomes. For two decades individuals and organizations have hired me for this expertise and reaped huge rewards for the effort. It is the place where strategy meets possibilities and when there are possibilities everyone is happier and more productive.

I implore everyone to be in pursuit of simple ideas. If you are lucky enough to find an idea that is a great fit, then be encouraged that with the right fuel and a smart direction you will be on the road to finding your awesome.

PART 1

SERIOUSLY, HOW DID I END UP HERE?

CHAPTER 3

THE REALITY PARADIGM

From almost the time we are born, there is a strong desire to conform to what other people think. We are ingrained with thoughts and preconceived notions of what "will work" and what "won't work." The problem with this is we are giving away our power and turning our values and abilities over to someone else to define what will work for us.

It takes bold courage to hold onto your power or take it back if you have given it away. We typically learn from an early age what is possible for ourselves. We learned this through a combination of societal norms, culture, gender and race biases, genetics, and circumstances of our lives. For the most part, our morals reflect our cultures, trends and sensibilities. Different societies have different ideas of what is and what isn't acceptable.

I grew up in a middle class blue-collar family in Ontario, Canada. Both parents worked in what would be considered the cultural norm for the sixties and seventies eras. My Dad was an appliance service technician and proudly worked for the same company for 35 years. My mother was employed as an administrative assistant in the healthcare industry for over 20 years. Neither parent ever stepped out of their cultural comfort zone. They were raised to play it safe, pay cash for everything and save money for their retirement.

My mother took care of all the household responsibilities, such as cooking, cleaning, shuffling me to my various activities and the general child rearing of my sister and myself. That was very stereotypical of the era I was raised in as my father worked long hours and managed a large work territory.

My mother was essentially the boss. She was the CEO of our household managing both her full time job and our family. Although it might have been tiring for her, she made it all look so easy, modeling what responsibility, consistency and love looked like.

Despite the cultural and societal norms of the time, my parents always encouraged me to ignore any naysayers and go after what I was dreaming of whether or not it conformed to society. I was so fortunate to be raised by parents who instilled the idea that I could do anything if I worked hard!

Although admittedly, I often dreamed of being raised in a more affluent family and in a better part of town, I realize now that I was never stifled by my blue-collar middle class upbringing or that I was a female. Those societal views never played into our conversations. Instead my parents instilled their full confidence and belief in the fact that I could achieve whatever I set my mind to. This infusion of confidence and validation from my parents and even from grandparents allowed me to dream about possibilities for my life.

Through the years I have created and accepted many new opportunities, which enabled me to develop skills, abilities and knowledge that I would not have had if I had grown up in a different family. For example, I was never held back by society's perceptions of what a young middle class girl, growing up on the east side of the city should do.

There were no preconceived ideas or any familial beliefs of being less fortunate or having less opportunity simply due to where I lived or what my gender was. It is because of my family that I was taught to work hard and put in my time and then my dreams would become a reality.

While I was unaware at the time, this mindset set the stage for big dreams and high expectations of myself. The responsibility I felt for building an amazing life brought me back to the day I graduated from high school with the feeling of exuberance, excitement and big plans for my future. I wanted a lot out of life and therefore that meant, in my mind, I had to work very hard all the time to ensure I was moving towards those goals.

My personal mantra and that of my reputation became something of a supergirl, who would grow into a superwoman who excelled at literally everything I did. Without even knowing it, as a young child, I created my own cultural norm, a norm that I felt immense pressure from all the time. I carried this pressure with me even into adulthood.

They say that your biggest strength is often your biggest weakness as well. This is mine. If I don't come first or win at everything I try, I feel like I didn't work hard enough...because if I had, I would have won.

THE CULTURAL CLASH

Years ago my husband and I hosted international students in our home. We would house two students at a time from various countries and they would live with our family in three to six month increments so they could better master the English language. There was one particular Asian student who stands out in my memory as he holds the record for one of the most humorous moments in our role of being a host family.

It was an event where expectations clash with reality and what he thought was the norm really wasn't. This young man, a junior executive with Toyota, came to Canada to better his English language skills and to learn about our North American culture.

In anticipation of his arrival, I prepared his room with some fresh linens, information about our country, our city and some gifts of memorabilia from our family. We were all excited about his impending arrival and we waited with anticipation. On this particular day our new guest arrived at our home by shuttle.

My husband and children welcomed our new guest into our home first as I made my way from the kitchen to do the same. Normally in North American culture, we would say "hello," "welcome" or "nice to meet you" followed by the shake of hands or a hug as gesture of hospitality. What happened in this moment was something different and even now all these years later brings a smile to my face.

With excitement and trepidation of his first English greeting he opened his mouth and looked my way and asked, "How old are you?" and "How much you weigh?" Imagine my surprise as I fully processed what he just said; shock on my face and utterly at a loss for words for a moment. My husband had to step away, feigning a cough as he started laughing with tears glistening in his eyes.

Honor and respect was of utmost importance to our young guest, and we knew his heart was in the right place. He desperately wanted to impress us and make a huge first impression, yet in just a few words he missed the mark on one of his first attempts to assimilate into North American culture. In his culture those types of questions at a first impression meeting were completely normal and very much expected.

The common questions that someone from his background was expected to ask were, "How much do you make?" "Are you married?", "You're fat." "Do you have kids?" and "Did you have lunch?" Knowing his heart was in the right place and he was trying so hard to make good relations, I graciously smiled and said, "Nice to meet you too." I later learned through one of my more cultural savvy friends and an English as a second language professor that the polite answer to all of those questions was a simple, "yes."

Once our student's English had improved a little and he had time to get acclimatized to our country, I started with some lessons to teach him how to properly greet people in our culture. He quickly picked up North American cultural norms and expectations and began his own journey to assimilate into it. This was a rather humorous example of how cultures can clash and how expectations don't always match reality. The same can said for assimilating into someone else's standards besides you own.

BELIEVE IN YOUR AUTHENTIC SELF

Through cultural avenues we learn what is socially acceptable. In the lighthearted example about our international student you can easily see how societal differences can make for some humorous situations. All of our experiences throughout our lives mean something and have an impact whether we want them to or not. The reality is that those early experiences in life whether it be people, places and expectations make an imprint, playing a major role in how we perceive ourselves in this world.

In many areas of our lives those experiences and the wisdom gained from them give us a foundation that sets the tone for how we will contribute as an adult in future years. It is when we fail to challenge our perspective and hold tight to our limiting beliefs that it becomes a potential red flag and a possible detriment to our future success.

A good example is how many of us enter into adulthood as people pleasers and in adult years we judge our own worth by how others may see us. If the right person doesn't see value or potential in us, we take their word for it and never go after what truly makes us happy.

AUTHENTIC SELF

The journey to bold courage is about finding satisfaction and happiness in who you are. I challenge you to claim your authentic self and forget about other people's standards; the only standard that counts is the one you set for yourself. I am not saying run out and break laws and fling dirt in the face of societal conformity. Rather, I'm saying it's time to give yourself permission to become more authentically you.

Allow your voice to be heard and allow your dreams, beliefs and desires to be the ones that dictate how you live your life and make decisions. Keep in mind that other people around you will have different values and ideals defined by their life experience because every person is unique. We each have different beliefs and wants from life.

It is time to believe. Believe in yourself and stop worrying what others will think. You may worry that you weigh too much or too little, or that you are too frugal with money or too frivolous, that you are too boring and conventional or that you are considered wild with huge pipe dreams of what you will do. Believe in your own standards before anyone else's.

It's time for you to get out of your own way and stop judging yourself by other people's standards. Standards may vary from society to society, but you don't have to accept them all just because the people around you do. Nor should you expect others to conform and believe in your standards. It doesn't mean either set of standards is wrong or lacking in moral fiber. Just respect each other and move on to what you really want to do.

Only you know what is right for you. Honoring your values and pursuing your goals with intentions are the keys to honoring your authentic self. This takes bold courage to find your truth, to confidently step forward into the calling on your life no matter the ridicule, guilt or shame that you may be feeling.

Seeing value in yourself is the anchor to confident living. Believing in yourself, your ability to make decisions and aligning your big goals with daily actions will get your far in your journey. Self-worth is the anchor to honoring your truest potential and authentic self.

You will be influenced by what society tells you and by your surroundings. However, you can choose to accept or deflect that influence. We all create our own expectations of ourselves; some people have extremely high expectations and others go the opposite way and underestimate themselves and have limiting beliefs. From either side of the coin it takes courage to step outside of your thought patterns and really examine the potential inside of you.

Take a walk through the garden of your thoughts. Identify the most important values that you want to use as guideposts on which to base your future decisions. Once you identify those values, your ideas will become clearer and your overarching vision will start to align into a reality. It is important to honor yourself and your beliefs in this way to begin to find your authentic self, or to reinforce what you already know.

THE ROAD TO AMAZING

In the journey to honoring the passion that I want to have in my life and the process of learning to live a more intentional life, I went looking for something. I got lost in the hustle and bustle of striving for greatness. I got lost in the societal views of how my success is defined. Without even realizing it, I was caught up in the notion that I needed to make so much money, or have a certain title, or dress and look a certain way to have value.

Even though my upbringing taught me that I could do anything, I realized I still based my judgment of success not on anything I innately knew to be true, but on everything society told me was important. I thought all I had to do was work hard to get more money and buy more stuff. In the journey of honoring my values and dreams I was reminded how quickly I could stray away from my own ideals. That was an important recognition for me.

From the outside looking in, I was a success story. I had achieved financial success, made a difference in communities, won numerous accolades and acquired prestige beyond what most would imagine. Yet, somehow I felt unfulfilled in my life and kept striving for more. I felt that I couldn't stop and smell the roses. I realized that I was living life by other people's standards. I was striving for things because I could, and not necessarily because I wanted them or felt any passion for them.

To most people, this doesn't matter; but it did to me. I wanted my life to mean something. I know I have a bigger purpose on this earth and it is my challenge to figure out what that is.

Suddenly I recognized that my hunger to make a difference in this world was getting bigger and with my child-like faith and big bold dreams I wanted to do something of major impact. I started to ask myself the question, "What would my lasting legacy look like?" "How could I leave a lasting imprint on this world long after I am gone?"

I searched like a prospector for that nugget of gold as I worked with individuals, organizations and communities. I needed to uncover what was so awesome for me that I could grab my bold courage and get going. In my zeal I learned something about the process of becoming more intentional with my calling.

Rushing and panicking don't help you find your purpose; you need to be still and allow the clarity to fill in the silence. I needed to listen to that inner voice and to wait in faith that my direction would be unveiled and I'd be set on a path with a purpose that makes sense. What a journey I was in for!

PART 1

SERIOUSLY, HOW DID I END UP HERE?

CHAPTER 4

THE PACE YOU TRAVEL

The thing about being still and learning to trust is that it sounds easy, but for a driven woman who wants to take on the world, that process has proven to be the part of my leadership journey that I would call prickly. It's like watching a flourishing rose bush in full bloom with the most beautiful of fragrant flowers, but covered in little thorns that sting when they prick you. Roses have always been revered for their beauty and the purpose of the thorns on a rose bush is to protect them from any dangers that might threaten their existence. I started thinking about what I believed in that might be threatening my dreams for my future.

Learning to get off the tight deadline race, release current and past disappointments and sit quietly alone has been a gift. It has created time to allow for new ideas or solutions to present themselves. This process has proven to be illuminating and simultaneously challenging. It has allowed my ability to dream to enter into a new phase of boldness.

During that time I was able to release all notions of self-induced barriers and failures and allow my dream to unfold in a new way through my open mind. The simple definition of the word dream, according to

Merriam-Webster, is a series of thoughts, visions, or feelings that happen during sleep. It is an idea or vision that is created in our imagination and it is not real. Further to that a second definition of the word dream is a strongly desired goal or purpose.

For me, anchoring my purpose has been one of the keys to me feeling validated and whole. It also gives me clarity about the next best steps to take and I make decisions that are aligned with that purpose. The process of connecting dreams to a purpose makes the process and work seem so much easier.

THE LONG RACE

As a young track athlete I was always a sprinter. I loved the quick burst of energy and the fast pace of the race and I consistently ranked in the top five in my age class. However, my desire was to be a cross country runner, having the strength and endurance to continue on a long road, running against the elements and still keeping a steady flow of air as my breathing supported my physical exertion. The picture of the marathoner or long distance achiever has always stayed in my head and to this day I still dream of running that long race.

Maybe it's because in my mind, I have never been able to run a full marathon like the sprinter inside of me wanted to. Somehow my mindset has kept me on this short track sprint, running as fast as I can, like a trajectory rather than an athlete setting a pace in a long race and ensuring that his or her body and mind can handle it. Only in the last few years have I realized that through my career thus far, I have tried to run the short sprint pace and made decisions based on that mindset versus a longer term thought process and running the long race pace.

Because of my sprint mentality, I was getting tired of everything. Every hurdle seemed like a brick wall covered in spikes that I couldn't scale. Upon realizing this, I started to challenge my thinking when it came to taking action on my dreams and setting the right strategy for success.

DREAMS ARE MEANT TO BE LIVED

We have all had dreams that didn't work out in our lives. I am no different than anyone else in that regard. I've had dreams that crashed and burned, and some that faded quietly to the background. I've had dreams that I changed my mind about and pushed off the cliff. There is no shame in attempting to realize a dream and for one reason or another having it not come true. Nothing ever feels good about our dreams being dashed, but when we let go and free ourselves for the next inspiration, our true passion can shine.

Many famous people are forthright about their failures. Albert Einstein couldn't speak fluently until he was nine. Steve Jobs was fired from the company he founded. Bill Gates dropped out of Harvard.

One of the most eloquently described failures is Harry Potter book author J. K. Rowling, who shared the experience in a commencement address at Harvard University.

She said she failed on an epic scale. Her short marriage failed, her job ended, and she was a single parent alone and poor in Britain. In her own words, she was the biggest failure she knew.

Most high profile leaders that I have interviewed proclaim to have had far more failures than successes. Their collective advice is to always get back up and try again. They shared that with the right perspective and some perseverance people can choose to overcome their fears.

Upon reflection of their advice I came to a revelation. We, as leaders of our own lives, need to raise the bar and commit to action despite fear. Our dreams need to be big enough, crazy enough, and daring enough to spark urgency and passion. Our dreams are meant to be lived and not placed high up on a shelf collecting dust only to be taken down to look at on special occasions like the family china on a milestone birthday.

When you combine dreaming with passion and urgency you have all the ingredients to set an idea in motion. A dream devoid of passion or urgency is just another idea. Possibly it is another good idea that you can look at for the future, but for now it will take a back burner to one more urgent. Gaining perspective on any dream or idea is critical and can lead you to success.

Learning to do a check in with my perspective as I made plans has been key to setting a smart pace for connecting my dream to strategy and for bringing it to reality.

DISRUPTION IS A PART OF DREAMING

For more than twenty years I have been an entrepreneur and have learned to rise and fall with the punches. From acquisitions to failures, and to award winning success my emotions have run deep and my passions have been pushed to the limits. The truth is, having the courage to dream also comes with its share of disruptions and the risk of failure. Disruptions are those little things (or big things) that happen along the way to realizing your dream that interrupt the momentum and steal your confidence. They slow your momentum.

Disruption on its best day is rarely welcomed and in the case of dream building, it is often one of the key troublemakers to signal a failed plan. You will come up against many obstacles in your journey to bold courage and the life you want to live and you need to be prepared. Disruptions and distractions won't sink your dream ship, but your reactions to them will if they aren't handled smartly.

The best defense against disruption is to find clarity in your destination. A dream cannot be pursued by anyone if they don't know where they want to go. The journey from inspiration to action and then figuring out how to pivot and evolve along the way is a skill that will continue to be refined if practiced. You have to think about it with some strategy attached.

In order to see your dream through and realize achievement there are always key elements that need to be present. The visionary sets the stage with the big dream. It is within this dreaming process that an idea of who, what, when, where, and why are answered. The how is in the planning. How we approach situations or tackle solving problems is where we can easily be sidetracked and taken on a different path.

[1]The Statistic Brain Research Institute showed some interesting findings between their 2015 and 2000 respective studies on attention span. In 2015, the average person has an attention span of 8.25 seconds. This has been greatly reduced by 3.75 seconds from the 2000 study showing 12 seconds of attention span. This study is a shocking reminder that in today's competitive marketplace, you are more likely to win by strategically figuring out how to manage your ability to focus.

Learning to focus among major distraction is essential to finding happiness, success, great productivity and bottom line results. When the vision connects to a plan and the plan is easy to take action on regardless of distractions or sidebars in your day, you know without a doubt what needs to get done and you make it a priority to do so. To keep a dream alive is to give it all you've got and to figure out a way, even when everything seems impossible.

DREAM DISRUPTION OVERLOAD

Wow! What a day it was. It certainly wasn't the most shining or productive of days. I was actually feeling quite out of sorts. I was in the midst of a demanding schedule and racing to a deadline with the technology company that I spoke of earlier in Chapter 1. Times were stressful and mind stretching, and the sheer number of decisions and considerations on my plate shook my confidence to a new low. I was at a point of serious fatigue and but still I pushed for more from myself.

I aimed for success and dreamed of a smooth place of momentum, yet at every turn I felt disrupted and hit with one more disappointment

---

1   The Statistic Brain Research Institute 2015 Study www.statisticbrain.com

Chapter 4

and one more deadline. There were so many milestones to celebrate, yet I didn't give that a priority. Instead I focused on those things that discouraged me and that weren't perfect. I was defeated by the many disruptions and imperfections and had an attitude of resignation.

I considered that I wasn't smart enough to make the company succeed and that my dreams were not going to come true. The feeling of defeat did not sit well with me, in fact, it was crushing me. There were so many people depending on the success of this venture and I felt responsible for it all. My spirit was at an all-time low, my belief in myself hit rock bottom and my self-loathing was at an all-time high.

When I look back now, I can see I was accomplishing great things and having huge personal growth, but at the time my judgment was clouded by the disruptions that seemed endless. It was fairly easy to ward off the self-doubt when there were just one or two disruptions over a time period.

But remember, my business was like a marathon but I was running it at a sprinter's pace. I was extremely tired and the disruptions came at me quickly and soon they became hurdles that seemed higher and higher making it harder to clear them with each passing challenge.

Small things that happened became large things when experienced at the speed I was running.

Have you ever played one of those children's video games where you drive the race car through ordinary streets and have to avoid obstacles and at starter speed it's easy, but once you gain race car driver speed, a simple obstacle can cause your car to wreck? That was me. I was going at a speed that I couldn't see the obstacles clearly anymore and they began to pile up on the bumper of my racecar.

Years ago, during this same time period, there was one such disruption I remember that knocked me off my game. I was meeting with a respected male businessman who was mentoring me. He challenged me on every level and rather than feeling uplifted like most mentor relationships, I often felt rather inadequate after meeting with him.

My team's code name for him was Grand Master Puff Daddy. You know the type. He liked to spout off his brilliance and judgment on everything even when he had no real experience with what he was talking about. Nonetheless, he felt he had to be right and wanted to weigh in on every subject. That one particular day, he weighed in on the technology sector and more specifically my technology company. He told me a male should be in charge of my company instead of me. He felt that a male would portray a better story and that I simply was not capable of the job although it wasn't my fault entirely because I was a woman. He shared that a man would be a better figurehead for all purposes involved with the company.

I was shaken to the core, as I had no idea what he was seeing and immediately felt like a failure even though I had won numerous awards previously as an entrepreneur. This disruption made me question everything about myself (apart from my gender) and that made it harder and harder to make decisions. It was then that the disruptions really started to pile up. As my belief in my role as CEO of my company waivered I started to believe I would never be good enough, and apart from gender reassignment there wasn't anything I could do about it.

From that point on, I started to believe that everyone was seeing me the same way, as incapable, inept, inadequate, and ineffective so I started to close off my circle. I started being busier and less social. I used my busy schedule as a cloak to protect me against having close relationships with anyone.

BLESSINGS FOUND IN DISRUPTION

The road to success is sometimes a lonely one, but it doesn't have to be. One of the most exciting things about dreams (other than achieving them) is when you find someone who believes in the dream too. If you can find someone who believes in your dream enough to join you on the journey it is extremely validating and it's a whole lot less lonely. It

Chapter 4

naturally becomes easier to take the bumps and navigate the disruptions and much more fun to celebrate the victories! The old adage rings true about there being strength in numbers.

Over the years many people came and went in my respective companies. The quest to find loyal and talented people to work with is always paramount. I was fortunate to find someone who joined my firm who believed in my company, the solution I was trying to build, but most importantly, someone who believed in me.

With my confidence iffy at best, it was a comfort to have a colleague by my side to help me weather the storms of disruptions that felt like a nearly everyday occurrence. Having someone else who believed helped put the lows into perspective so they didn't seem so crushing and made the highs that much higher as we celebrated every chance we got!

Through the years and through thick and thin that particular colleague stood by me the whole way and became an essential leader in my firm. She was as driven as I was and never took her eye off the goal. She remained loyal to me through many trials and tribulations, where it would have been so much easier for her to quit. I often wondered why she stayed because it wasn't easy and many times we barely escaped being washed down the drain like so many other technology start-ups. Still, she remained by my side and we worked hard to support each other and the rest of our team through our fears and to keep momentum and morale moving forward.

On my more fearful days I commiserated about what my mentor had said to me when he said I was unsuitable to be the CEO of my own company. I would chastise myself for being perceived as anything less than fully equipped to handle myself, to be respected and lead my company in a male dominated industry.

My self-loathing would ramp to levels that would overcome my ability to see the positive in the journey. On one such day, I arrived to my office to find a card addressed to me on my keyboard.

I opened the card to find it was a hand written card from that colleague who had been standing by me for so long. I caught my breath as I started to read the words as I half expected it to be a resignation letter. What I read was quite the opposite; it was a letter of encouragement for me. I continued reading the note from my friend with the feeling that I was so undeserving.

She wrote from her heart and shared with me all the ways I had inspired her over the last number of years and told me all of the things she had learned from me. The note was so raw and written with such clarity that I was dumbfounded.

It was the moment that I realized that the journey had had difficult moments, but was made so much easier because I had surrounded myself with great people. I realized that I wasn't alone. I had people in my life who were willing to share the journey and actually wanted to be part of my crazy adventure, no matter the outcome. What started as a day of feeling "less than" ended on a note of recognition and blessing.

After reading that message, I must have been a sight. I was totally taken back and shocked by her sweet note, I proceeded to stare and take in all that she had shared. I started to reflect on how people see me and why it is so different than how I see myself. I later asked her the question. "You really see me this way?" To which she just smiled with a knowing grin and answered, "of course."

She then shared that every one of those points in the note were qualities that she had been watching and mentoring from for a long time. It was clear to me on that day that disruptions were no match for loyalty and teamwork. Her years of loyalty and support and then the subsequent note brought about hope in me again. I began to consider and see myself through her eyes and that gave me a new drive to keep going.

Travelling the road to my dream was much more efficient by having others who believed in me. To have a colleague who was at risk of not getting paid but still wanted to keep going was a gift I will always remember. I found renewed strength in the pride and determination to not let anyone else or myself down. I realized then that although someone else thought I was amazing, I needed a reset. Suddenly I felt a bit empowered and wanted to be able to see myself through my own eyes the way she saw me through hers.

PART 1

SERIOUSLY, HOW DID I END UP HERE?

CHAPTER 5

THE CASE FOR BOLD COURAGE

If there has ever been a time in recent history that there is a need to re-engage the human spirit it is now. Our world is changing. There is a silent shift happening, one that you may not be able to see but you can certainly feel.

Through my years of research with both individuals and organizations, I've seen that people are restless, jittery and on many levels uncomfortable with their lives and they want change. I was not surprised this year when Gallup Research released their poll that showed only one third of workers actually feel engaged in their workplace.

Not only do people want change, they are demanding change. Often times they are looking for big change, whether it be in their jobs, their relationships, their family, their finances or even where they live. People are hungry for more in their lives and want to feel fulfilled and confident in themselves and their life's journey. They are tired of feeling afraid, resigned and full of regret. Most times people don't know where to start to make change and get overwhelmed. Sound familiar?

The 21st century is considered the knowledge age. This has shifted the way people seek, process and share information. This century has ushered in a new way of thinking, both individually and collaboratively as a team. There is now a demand for a continual flow of communication, ideas and of evolution of thought in all areas of life. People have a new understanding about what it means to be global, capable and impactful. There are more people wishing and dreaming about doing things of great impact and who are no longer content to rely on large corporate structures to make it happen.

People are more willing to risk, have increased faith to see a plan through, and the tenacity to give it all they've got. There is an uprising of civic mindedness happening. We have a need to make an impact and do something more with life rather than just exist to go to work and pay bills.

I share all of this with you to assure you that you are not alone in your search for a more fulfilled life. The desire to make change is your starting point. Congratulations on the first step. Celebrate the fact that you have made the decision and that you are ready! Having bold courage is the next step. Bold courage is about shifting your perspective, discovering your possibilities, making the decision to take risks and learning to play a bigger game in life.

> Bold courage is about shifting your perspective, discovering your possibilities, making the decision to take risks and learning to play a bigger game in life.

DO WHAT IS RIGHT, NOT JUST EASY

Bold Courage is about committing to action despite your fear. It is about becoming more disciplined in your approach to living and working with an engaged and renewed sense of excitement, accomplishment, and joy. When you recognize the sheer importance of your daily actions and the attitudes in which you do those actions, you lay the foundation for your continued success or failure. With the right approach you also insulate and protect yourself against those daily disruptors that try to steal your confidence.

A SIMPLE FOCUSED PLAN

The pursuit of greatness and the act of accomplishing great things is a dream of many. Over the course of my career, I have met thousands of people who reflect on their lives with regrets of chances never taken and dreams never fulfilled. Many people spend their whole life struggling to come to terms with what could have been. Through them I repeatedly saw this trend and my heart hurt for those people and their disappointment.

The good news is that with a healthy dose of bold courage and the decision to live more intentionally they would avoid future regrets.

Bold Courage was born out of my own personal call to action to change my life for the better. In the process I realized that everyone could benefit from its principles. Thousands of people are living in a place of brokenness, where fear, disappointment, uncertainty, and feelings of inadequacy have taken hold. This is apparent in many areas, but most dramatically in the workplace where we see the substantial rise of mental health cases, disability claims, and the negative impact on productivity in the workforce.

To help people get back on track to finding their awesome, I developed a new boldness strategy for life. It is a simple and focused plan of action for conquering daily achievements that is consistent, repeatable and aligned to owning your awesome in a bigger way. It is the big dream connected to small, every day actions that achieves the most long-lasting results. It is about using what you innately have control over, which is your attitude, skills, abilities, passions, hobbies and talents, and pairing them with opportunities to allow the authentic you to shine through.

Imagine what would happen if we all took ownership of our own lives and started committing to do the right things, with the right attitude with the right people in our midst. I wanted to create that scenario in my life as much as I could as I saw a great foundation for a fulfilled and satisfied life.

WHY I CHOSE BOLD COURAGE

I wanted to be bolder in my life. I didn't feel as fulfilled as I wanted and I craved more. Other people saw me as an inspiration in life and I had been told many times that people admired my life and held it in high regard as something they aspired to have. But I didn't hold it high like them. I saw myself as someone who was stuck on a merry go round that I couldn't get off. Although I had found success in many areas, I knew I had somehow accepted less than my awesome in others.

There were some areas of my life that were lacking and I knew it. I had to make some decisions and pair it with a smart action plan to kick my proverbial butt to get up, stop sabotaging myself, and fulfill the dreams I set out long ago, not to mention a few more I decided to add to the list. I wanted to live my passion and impact the lives of others in a more positive way. This meant defining what awesome meant to me. In this instance it meant intentionally articulating what my ideal lifestyle looked like, what it felt like and how exciting it would be to actually live it.

For me, it was learning to identify and be more intentional in how I use my strengths, my passions and how I use my authentic voice. I've always had a desire to achieve something of lasting legacy-building impact in both my life and in my career. It was this desire that fueled my bold courage and how I later discovered that finding and owning my awesome would change everything.

MY AWESOME DEFINED

I identified a few segments of my life in which I wanted to see and experience improvements. The first was my relationship with my family. While I adored my family, I craved a deeper connection. That meant setting priorities around building memories together and having meaningful conversations to deepen our relationships with each other.

The second segment was health and I wanted to own my awesome health and that meant tackling some bad habits and dealing with some recurring health issues that were disrupting my lifestyle. I craved strength, energy and vibrancy and I was lacking in all of those areas. However, I was excited to do something about it and hopeful to achieve the improvements I desired.

The third segment was in business and career, I committed to owning my awesome in business and that meant taking the time to look at everything from operations, to people, to our product and service offerings, and even to the types of customers with whom we would choose to work.

Nothing was sacred during this process. I put everything on the table as I started to lead my shift to owning my awesome again. Because I believed in myself, the magic started to happen. That day I started challenging myself to face my fears and disappointments head on. I started being honest with myself and I put words to the feelings that were crippling my life and holding me back.

The irony of the entire situation is that from an external view I was completely successful, busy and continuing to accomplish significant things. That was all true, but I knew I was missing an important part for me. It was a matter of the heart, knowing that my heart and soul had somehow disconnected from what I was doing. Once I recognized that fact it became easier to take steps to change my situation.

ALIGN FOUR CATEGORIES

Through my research and test studies, I discovered that there are four key categories to consider when you decide to journey to own your awesome. If you focus on the core understandings within each category you will be able to create consistency, alignment and repetition in your efforts and therefore in your success.

Consider consistency, alignment and repetition as the vehicle you will use to get you to your destination of owning your awesome. Consider the fuel for your tank to be the categories and the six- step process of the Success Tracker System, (which you will learn about later). All four categories play an equal and integral role in helping you reach your awesome so you can own every inch of your life.

Within each category there are a few core understandings that will help you in your journey.

1. Commitment
    » Be willing to take your commitment to the next level.
    » Be willing to try new things.
    » Be committed to trust in the process.
    » Be committed and okay with being uncomfortable.
    » Recognition
    » Recognize the beauty of failing.
    » Recognize the need to embrace chaos.
    » Understand the process of winning.
    » Recognize that by doing just one thing you can change your world.

2. Satisfaction
    » Challenge mediocrity.
    » Recognize the power of your story.
    » Accept being perfectly flawed.
    » Understand the gift of giving and receiving.

3. Feedback
    » Become empowered through feedback.

- » Use feedback as a launch pad.
- » Gain resiliency through feedback.
- » Foster communication in relationships.

Bold Courage is a call to arms to claim you're awesome. It is a challenge to you, right now, to commit to stop the whining and self-pity about your life and commit to doing a reset. Renew your attitude and adjust your actions and in just a few weeks you will start to see the changes that you have been waiting for. It's up to you; the best time to start is now.

PART 2

THE SEARCH FOR SIGNIFICANCE

CHAPTER 6

A WORLD OF RELEVANCE

Living in a lifestyle of bold courage requires commitment to the goal of owning your awesome. The level of your commitment is directly connected to the level of success you will achieve.

That means setting a priority that the journey to owning your awesome is not only significant but will be held to the highest level of importance. Consider owning your awesome a marathon of sorts. It is a rare occasion that anybody running a marathon crosses the finish line without first having committed to running the race.

When you are ready to step forward and claim a life of owning your awesome, the commitment you make to the process of getting there is critical. Commitment is the foundation from which you will set your goals and measure every activity. It is a crucial component of your personal leadership development that allows you to build a new disciplined approach to living and working with excellence.

Consider this a discipline of taking your commitment to the next level. It is an earnest pledge to achieving greatness. You know that even when things are difficult, you will stay on track and follow through to the end. Committing to set priorities makes a world of difference because doing the right actions at the right times aligned with the right focus will always help you stay on track to your goal.

As you commit to yourself and your journey there is a level of emotional and intellectual dedication to the process. When you are dedicated to something and have a direct stake in the outcome, you are far more likely to be committed to doing what needs to be done to get there. Your actions must match your words and when they do there is nothing that can stop you.

In the Star Wars movie, *Return of the Jedi,* the character Yoda said it best when he spoke to the young Jedi, Luke Skywalker during his training, explaining, "Do or do not. There is no try." The same can be said for your commitment to bold courage. You are either committed or you're not; there is no grey area. You can't be a little bit committed and stay on track. You need to be all in. Being committed takes personal discipline and a stick-to-it attitude that will be challenged many times as you progress naturally through plenty of doubts.

As you make commitments you are making promises to yourself to follow through with your plan. Before making a firm commitment to anything it is a good idea to be crystal clear on the desired outcome. What will the path to get there look like? We often live life with no clear goal of where we want to get to and thus feel like our life is made up of just going to work and paying bills.

As a leadership expert and business strategist, it has always amazed me that a person will take so much time and energy to envision and create an engaging and results oriented business plan, but take no time to consider their life plan and what their offering to the world could be.

If we approached our life planning like a business plan we would set goals a lot differently. We would highlight our best offering, in this case our strengths, and our ideal market, those people who enjoy spending time with us and whom we enjoy spending time with.

We would identify how much money we need for our life and figure out the best roads to take in order to get it. Like a business plan, we would also market or promote ourselves and we would be confident to share and celebrate our successes along the journey of life. In the process, we would inspire others and lead them.

As the quality control manager behind our plans we would always measure the success of our big vision so we would know we were on always on the right track. Wouldn't it be interesting if life always worked out that way? Most times it doesn't, but it could.

The only way to know that you are achieving progress in your quest to own your awesome is to have a plan that you can commit to and measure your milestones. Getting clear about your destination is essential so that you can align your decisions and actions. A commitment to owning your awesome is a solemn promise to yourself to create the life you desire. Bold courage is the vehicle to get you there.

> As a leadership expert and business strategist, it has always amazed me that a person will take so much time and energy to envision and create an engaging and results oriented business plan, but take no time to consider their life plan and what their offering to the world could be.

DEFINING AWESOME

Fitting commitment into a work/life balance structure can be extremely difficult and create an unnecessary frustration to make the "balance." Work life balance is outdated and something I have quite honestly never believed in. Our lives can get complicated with the never-ending juggle of personal responsibilities including our work, family, community and extracurricular activities.

The fact is there never seems to be enough hours in the day and without having the luxury of adding more hours, the best we can do is manage what we have.

A traditional life coaching wheel has eight different segments to manage which includes; personal growth, physical environment, work and career, money, romance, friends and family, fun and recreation and health and fitness. No one has ever proven to me that all eight segments can, or should, be equally balanced at the same time. What I have discovered and seen in the successful lives of thousands of clients is that each one of us has the capacity to develop a work life rhythm that makes sense to us personally. That means setting priorities that are important and relevant to the bigger picture and making decisions that are aligned with that vision.

When we develop a rhythm that is aligned with our vision it becomes easier to spot and attract more things that are relevant to our journey while deflecting those things that are mere distractions. As we develop the skill of making decisions as determined by their relevance to our goal, it allows for adaptability and flexibility and places priorities on certain segments, therefore releasing the burden of having to balance it all.

With this notion in mind there is no right or wrong rhythm to your life. There is no classified standard set of rules of engagement that apply to all life rhythms. As the leader of your own life, only you can set a rhythm for managing your time that is right for you. Choose one that aligns with owning your awesome and that allows you to lead with confidence, make decisions that are relevant and have everything aligned to the ultimate goal.

DEFINING RELEVANCE

Once you have defined what your awesome is, what it looks like, and how it might be reached through various actions, it is time to get ruthless with your clutter. Clutter is anything that is hanging around that is no longer relevant to your definition of awesome. From that point on, each step and every action in your journey must be weighed against your desired outcome. Your actions should always be relevant to the path to your desired outcome.

Make the decision to eliminate anything in your life, your surroundings, and your mind that is just taking up space.

One of the major causes of stress and of time lost is the clutter we allow in our physical world and our mental world. This is not just the pile of paper on your desk at work, the junk drawer at home, or overflowing bins in your garage or closets. It also includes your thoughts.

As you strive to achieve a fulfilled and happy life of awesome, you will encounter some obstacles along the way. Some of these will be your own negative thoughts. This is completely normal. Living with bold courage requires you to clean up and clear away those objects and thoughts that are getting in the way and stopping you from focusing on what you really should be giving your attention to. Simply put, if it isn't relevant and helpful, get rid of it. By clearing away the clutter you make room for new and relevant ideas and solutions.

When thoughts and opportunities come your way, whether through your own creative mind or that of others, consider what will happen if you engage in them. That consideration will help determine if the thought is currently relevant to your situation or not. If you choose to do things that aren't relevant, you will be slowed down from your mission to achieve your awesome. You may even forget what you were committed to and wake up one day asking, "How did I get here?"

As opportunities arise, assess them. If they aren't relevant to your intended goal (or defined path to awesome), then put them down and let the opportunity pass you by. Opportunities are truly beneficial only if they help you achieve your intended goal. You will avoid a lot of clutter and wasted time if you are cognizant of how you spend your time.

As you know, one of my strong attributes is the ability to come up with a lot of ideas quickly. This also has given me some grief over the years. Grief because of this skill came in a couple of ways through my business. As I focused on honing my ideation skills, I sometimes would find myself actually creating problems where none previously existed simply to give me something to ideate about. This led to me off track and off task. I could find myself spending time on things that didn't really need attention, leaving me little time to focus on important things.

As I found new ideas they were all like shiny pennies glistening in the sunlight and I watched them sparkle. I do love things that sparkle and I love new ideas so this made a terrific combo for me! As much as this process makes me happy, I also recognize that if left unchecked this can be a distraction and is something I have learned to be aware of. I am careful to only ideate, innovate and consider opportunities that are in alignment with my goal of awesome. I certainly didn't take long to learn that lesson and can now immediately recognize when something doesn't match or connect directly or indirectly to my awesome. Aligning idea with goal now sets the stage to whether I should or should not put any further time into an idea.

Recognizing the relevance of the things we do and connecting it to the intended outcome is critical to being able to stay committed to your goal. When we do this it allows us to shift our thinking. Instead of stretching ourselves thinner by trying to get things all done and balancing everything, we can avoid increased stress and decreased productivity.

Set a plan to get laser focused on what truly needs your commitment and focus right now. Be committed to doing this all through your journey to bold courage. In order to find your awesome and claim it, you must be committed to staying on track and doing the things that need to be done to get there.

Commitment is one of four key components to develop a boldness strategy that can be sustained and built upon. By making commitments and conquering them it not only energizes us, but also engages us in the next challenge. With more conquering of tasks and further momentum generated towards your awesome, your self-confidence will grow and each decision will become easier than the last.

When we focus on those things that are relevant in our lives, we ready ourselves to solve problems, to serve others, and to be energized in our passion and vision. When we seek relevance to each task before us, we are more apt to reach out and engage with others, build teams and continually seek wisdom along the journey.

Relevance keeps you connected to the matter at hand and if that matter is the call to owning your awesome, then it makes sense that any commitments going forward should be measured against this plan. Choose those things that are considered relevant to the end game; owning your awesome. Let those items become your top priority every day.

PART 2

THE SEARCH FOR SIGNIFICANCE

CHAPTER 7

THE WILLINGNESS EFFECT

In 2009 I said yes to an opportunity that came my way. I was invited to sit on a global advisory council for women's issues for an international non-governmental charitable organization. The focus of the council was to discuss women's issues in developing countries ranging from disaster relief to health, food, water and education.

At the time, I had no idea where the opportunity would take me, except that I was hungry to use my skills to make a larger difference globally. My desire to play a larger role in helping others was at the forefront of my plan to own my awesome.

When the request came in, it would have been easy to say no. I was already busy with a ton of committees, often feeling overwhelmed with the hours in the day it took to fulfill my already hectic life. After all, I was already considered a successful entrepreneur with an extremely busy schedule to manage and simultaneously hosting a radio show and travelling the globe speaking professionally. Most people with my schedule might have said no to the offer right away and been done with it, recognizing that in an already hectic schedule adding one more commitment might not be the smartest idea.

Chapter 7

However, I however didn't make any snap decision. I took some time and thought to review how saying yes would align with my future goals. I considered the opportunity and its relevance to my life and even though I was busy, I imagined myself sitting on the committee and how it might feel and contribute to owning my awesome.

After my personal deliberation I wholeheartedly said yes and agreed to sit on the council. I dove into my new council position with willingness, excitement and the expectation of great things to come. I never do anything half way and this was no different; I was all in. As I always do, I did my research and prepared for my role on the advisory board, working hard to get up to speed on current strengths, weaknesses, opportunities and threats so that I could offer intelligent insight, ideas and a willingness to be open to finding smart solutions.

Due to the sheer number of initiatives being implemented it became clear that the best way to fully understand the impact of this organization would be to experience it firsthand. Six months later, I joined a team of seven other people (all strangers to me) and collectively we traveled to Africa, deemed as a country in need of rebuilding and restoration. Liberia, located in West Africa, is one of the poorest nations of the world, having suffered tremendously as a nation after surviving a horrific sixteen-year civil war and now most recently an Ebola outbreak. It is in the willingness to want to make a difference and help those in need that I joined this absolutely incredible organization and set forth to experience their meaningful work.

As I boarded the plane I admit that I felt a little shy being the only person in the group who didn't know the others. On top of that was travelling with them to a developing country leaving everything I knew behind. I had travelled many times by myself in the past, yet somehow this particular time I felt insecure.

Despite that, I knew that the success of this trip would come out of my willingness to play an active role in the group. It meant letting go of my insecurities and focusing on the incredible experience I was about to have. I was hungry to share my strengths, skills and abilities in any way they would be deemed useable and I knew I couldn't fully immerse myself into the experience if I remained in a state of shyness. My sights were set on global work and much to my awe and amazement, I was right where I always wanted to be. I crossed the threshold from dream to reality and was filled with gratitude.

I was ready to take the experience by the horns and give it my all, so I committed to myself to have the willingness to do whatever I had to do to immerse myself in the experience of the Liberian culture and support the team and the community any way I could. My willingness to be open to possibilities made all the difference. I thoroughly and completely enjoyed the entire experience and more than twenty-five projects, from startup ideas to massive countrywide initiatives.

I have always had an overachiever mindset, routinely setting the bar high for myself. This trip was no different and much to the chagrin of some of my teammates at times, I made myself available to join in and try everything and anything that came my way. I tried, led and connected with local people wherever I could (which to my delight was non-stop!). I took in every possible experience available on that trip, soaking it up, learning, understanding and comprehending the vision that was set out.

I wasn't leaving anything on the table. I wanted to have done it all. I spent my days doing a variety of things which ranged from playing games to singing, feeding 3,000 children in one day, being knee deep in a manure-fed tilapia pond learning to fish by hand, teaching literacy and hygiene classes in the middle of the jungle in a mud hut, building water systems, teaching entrepreneurship to women, and visiting a secured housing project that rescued young girls who had been sold into slavery as child soldiers during the war and later raped and abused.

The need was overwhelming and with a team of 600 in the nation, villages were being put back together and the road to healing had begun.

Saying yes to that experience and being willing to play an active part in it allowed me to return home feeling like I had found a piece of my awesome.

What started as a simple invitation to join an advisory council ended up launching me into a new era of stretching my potential and asking myself, "What else is possible?" Being open to amazing possibilities allowed me to reframe my idea of awesome and opened up a world of new thinking for successful living. This African experience helped me to put my awesome at the forefront, see opportunities and release any assumptions about what I thought this trip was going to be. I focused on the experience first and reflected on the learning after and came home a changed person. I learned to be more willing, more vulnerable and more grateful for everything I have.

OPEN TO INFINITE POSSIBILITIES

When you define your awesome, the possibilities are endless as to what that awesome can look like. Your awesome is only limited by your ability to consider possibilities to see yourself successful beyond what your current situation is. That means that regardless of your present state of affairs, you have to be willing to see possibilities and your potential for further greatness. The sky really is the limit when you are open to the myriad of opportunities around you and waiting to be discovered. As the famous Walt Disney said, "If you can dream it, you can do it."

I have followed this simple advice from Disney since I was a child and it really has brought about some fascinating opportunities for me. In my willingness to say yes and seek new possibilities, it has had a deep effect on my life, allowing me to keep dreaming big and being bold for the sake of my future. Having the willingness to dream and see the never ending potential for greatness is something I credit a large portion of my personal and business success to.

Another quote that I have always been fond of is from Henry Ford, founder of the Ford Motor Company who once said, "Whether you think you can or cannot, you're right."

Henry Ford was brilliant. He took every opportunity to look at new ways of thinking and learning and I have sought to do that throughout my life. In fact, Ford used his willingness to be open to invent some of the most groundbreaking developments in the automotive sector. He dreamed about where his business and industry could go and not where it currently was. His belief was that your mindset and willingness to see outcomes is critical to your success.

If you aren't willing to believe in yourself, you won't succeed. However if you are willing to believe in yourself, you will. Obviously it's not that simple and many things beyond your control can get in your way to success, no matter how much you believe you can succeed. It still comes down to asking yourself the questions: "Am I willing to believe that I can play a vital role in the success of my vision? Am I willing to make it happen and do I believe I am worthy of great things?"

In your journey with bold courage you must be willing to see yourself differently than your current circumstances present. If you aren't open to dreaming and seeing possibilities you will remain stagnant. Having the willingness to believe in your success sets the stage for committing to taking action toward that success. Willingness is quite possibly the most heroic word in the dictionary. It is where ordinary turns into extraordinary and where the human spirit shows its divine potential. Being willing to accept your potential and unlimited amount of awesome is often difficult and marred with challenges along the way.

Certainly for me, the hunger to make a difference and change the world is one that runs deep. I encourage you to get hungry about finding your awesome and have the willingness to strive to try new things and be open to new experiences. Be hungry for change, growth and impact and allow it to be the catalyst for becoming motivated to do something about it. With committed action, clarity of purpose and that burning desire to make a difference, you will do something of worth. It starts with willingness.

For much of my life, people have often remarked that they want to be more like me. They cannot understand how I have found the opportunities I have. Many think it was just luck, and maybe some of it was, but not all of it. I don't see myself in any way superior to anyone else intellectually or physically, but I have figured out that the difference with me really comes down to the idea of willingness. Because I wanted to create a bigger change in my life, my work, my relationships, my finances and my health, it came down to not only making the commitment but the willingness to take action at all cost.

Willingness separates you as a champion and sets the stage for those daily acts of personal courage that keep you moving toward your goal. Consider willingness as a posture or a mindset that commits to setting your plans in motion.

THE STARTING BLOCK

The award-winning sprinter is laser focused as he or she prepares for the finals of the 50-meter dash. They gaze down the track and with the finish line never out of sight they prepare their starter's stance. For the sprinter, this includes fitting one foot on a runner's block and aligning the rest of their body with the other knee bent at a 90 degree angle as the body stretches forward with both hands on the ground, fingertips poised to push off. This runner is now in the best possible position for the most successful start to his or her race. Willingness is like your starter's block allowing you to have the best possible starting position as you prepare yourself to launch.

Willingness is something you must commit to for the long haul. It is a lifestyle and not a one-time occurrence. This may require you to challenge your old thinking many times as you progress. It isn't always easy to shed doubts especially when they are about you, but it is possible.

Willingness often takes practice and you may catch yourself on some days digging your heels into old ways of thinking when it would be wiser to have willingness to be open minded and give way to new thinking. Don't be too hard on yourself. Instead, I encourage you to recognize the situation for what it is, which is nothing more than growing pains. With the right discipline, saying yes becomes a lot more fun than constantly saying no and later second-guessing yourself. Once you get the feel for it, willingness is quite addictive and saying yes becomes the norm.

PART 2

THE SEARCH FOR SIGNIFICANCE

CHAPTER 8

TRUST THE PROCESS

My childhood consisted of two seasons: when the swimming pool was open and when it wasn't. I loved swimming and every year I anxiously waited for when my father would announce that the day had arrived to take the winter cover off and officially open the pool for the season. From the early days of spring when the pool was first opened to the last cool evenings of fall when my father closed it, I relished swimming in that pool every single day. It was part of my daily routine and I became a great swimmer over the years and have the most wonderful memories of the many moments spent in that pool with my family.

I had a myriad of friends lining up who relished spending many days swimming at my house as well. It was not uncommon to spend the day playing and creating new water related games with whoever was with me that day which sparked a lot of laughter and enjoyment. One of the things I loved to do was swim underwater. I always found it a challenge to see how long I could hold my breath without having to come up for air.

When it came to the pool, my father was great fun and often challenged me to see how long I could swim underwater without coming up for air.

Years later I wondered if he was actually just looking for some peace and quiet around the pool for a minute and that by encouraging me to go underwater, he created his own peaceful moment, which was perhaps part of owning his awesome.

My father issued challenges to swim underwater laps back and forth and with each successful time he would up the ante and make it more challenging for me. I would swim as far as I could until my lungs hurt. Every time he called for a new challenge it would be met with excitement to make him proud and trepidation that it couldn't be done. I often feared I wouldn't be able to do it. But because it was my Dad making the challenge, I was willing to try it anyway. The challenge often seemed impossible to conquer, yet I would dive into the pool trusting that my lungs would carry me farther than the last time I attempted it.

As I took on whatever challenge was before me at the time, which at different moments included how many single leaves I could gather from the bottom of the pool in one breath, how many coins from the bottom I could collect, to swimming consecutive laps without a breath, I dove in and trusted my lungs could handle the workout. There were times when I didn't succeed on the first attempt and as I swam, I did everything I could to manage the air in my lungs to maximize my attempt and reach for a longer distance. Every time I took that deep breath before submersing myself, I trusted the process that my lungs would carry me where I needed to go. I couldn't scientifically calculate how much air I would need, nor could I measure how much air was in my lungs. I simply had to trust that I could make it back to the surface no matter how low my oxygen was.

I never really worried about whether I would survive my swimming excursions but always trusted my lungs to support my efforts even at those moments when I pushed it too far and desperately craved a breath. However, I do remember several times looking up from the bottom of the pool and feeling a sense of wonder as my lungs started to burn from lack of fresh air and as I pushed off the bottom I wondered if I would possibly make it to surface. My lungs got tighter and tighter on the way up when finally I broke the surface of the water and gasped to take in air.

For me, being able to continually dive deep underwater was directly reliant on my ability to trust that my lungs would always hold just enough air to get me back to the surface. Scientific proof and evidence weren't required, nor was it even possible, but to overcome my fear of running out of air, I had to have faith.

Faith is when you believe in something that you can't see, measure or prove beyond a shadow of a doubt that it even exists. Trust in the process of bold courage in your journey to owning your awesome is exactly the same. You will need to trust in the process of the journey even when your lungs are burning for air or you feel fearful that something isn't working or going well at the time.

As you journey it will be easy to doubt the process, doubt yourself and doubt your choices. There will be times when everything seems to be going wrong and you don't understand why and you will question the likelihood of success in your plan. All of that is completely normal and even expected.

Plans don't always go exactly as we dream them up, but knowing that the long-term process will work should give you courage and reassurance. Bold courage is not a sprint, but a marathon. There is no easy button or quick speed-up switch that will shoot you forward through any difficulties to reach your awesome faster.

Trusting in the process is a critical part of your journey. It requires believing in something bigger than yourself, something you cannot see. There is no hard-core scientific process that you can measure beyond a shadow of a doubt that it is working. You need to have faith that things are unfolding as they should and that you can handle anything that comes your way.

Having faith and trusting in the process is easy when things seem to be going your way and you can see the clear path to success. When things get hard and challenges rear up in your path and the path is not so clear, that is when you will need to trust the most. It takes bold courage to have faith in what you cannot see. Recognize that it is okay if you can't see every step of your journey. It is okay to not understand the process and to not have all the answers. The key thing is to commit to trusting the process and do the work required to continue moving forward in your quest for your awesome.

Trust doesn't require comprehension of everything; if it did our world would be in huge trouble. We place our trust and safety in the hands of others every day through teachers, police officers, food preparation staff, and auto mechanics, for example. We don't always know how to do something or have the time to do it so we place our trust and safety in others to do it for us. The process of using bold courage and owning your awesome is the same. Even though you may not understand every step, you must put your faith in the process and trust yourself and others as you move through it.

TRANSFORMATION TAKES TIME

As you trust in the process of bold courage, it is important to realize that transformation takes time. Change doesn't happen overnight and progress is often not as quick as we might like it to be. In society we tend to gravitate to instant gratification where we want to see the rewards for our efforts immediately. This isn't always the case. In fact, not only will there be times when you feel stagnant, there will be times when you will feel like you are moving backwards. That's normal too. Your journey is most likely not linear in nature nor can you map it with 100 percent accuracy.

Consider that lesson as part of your boldness strategy, trust the process as a period of change, growth and impact to get to your awesome.

You will see progress along the way, it is by no means instant, but the end reward is worth it. Your idea of awesome may even change as time passes. The only thing constant in life is change. Change is inevitable; it's how you view the change that matters.

Learning to manage and even thrive in the midst of change is not for the faint of heart. The difficult thing is that change doesn't discriminate. It presses everybody equally as hard as they will allow it. Whether you are walking through crisis, you want to lose weight, get in better physical shape, change careers or learn a new skill, you must realize that change is constant and it will require your focus, thought and determination to manage through it successfully. Your belief and trust in the process is critical.

You must know that although your situation may not be ideal in its current state, you can take comfort in the knowledge that things will get better. This includes having faith in spite of not knowing what the outcome will be, choosing to be wholly present throughout your journey, and living in the moment as you understand that bold courage will help you through the process.

Change and growth cannot happen when you stay in a place of what is known. When we choose to live only in places that are known to us we build a fortress in which we hide from any challenges. Opportunities pass by outside the walls we have erected. Bold courage encourages you to live in the place of the unknown for at least a time so you can experience and learn new ways to interact and contribute to the world.

Trust requires self-determination and tenacity. It requires you to rise above your own perceptions and negative thinking and have faith in the future. It is not living by chance but rather embracing the dreams of the future. When things get tough, hold that vision firmly in your mind. Renew your commitment to the now, being present and making sure you are pointed in the right direction with the right mindset as each day unfolds.

When we have bold courage and show willingness to trust the process of stepping into a bigger potential for our life, we also ready ourselves to brave those temporary storms, those times of discomfort and those seasons of uncertainty because the risk is worth the reward.

PART 2

THE SEARCH FOR SIGNIFICANCE

CHAPTER 9

BE UNCOMFORTABLE: BE BOLD WHERE YOU NEED TO BE

I can't put my finger on the exact moment it happened, but it most certainly did. I transformed from a relatively shy young woman to a woman described by others as knowledgeable, powerful, and influential. I had the ability to positively impact large numbers of people.

It may have started the day I had my first speaking engagement with a new speaker's bureau, one that I had worked diligently to build a relationship with and be represented by. This particular speaker's bureau had agreed to become an agent for me and this first booking was my opportunity to prove I was skilled, marketable and worth their team's effort to get me scheduled more often in the future.

The speaking engagement was a conference for human resource professionals with 600 professionals in attendance from all over the region. I was hired to speak on my concept of work life rhythm and the impact it can have on our leadership journey. I was well researched and prepared, I had the entire speech carefully crafted and scripted from start to finish.

All of my material was well branded and I even color-coordinated my outfit to match my PowerPoint presentation. I left nothing to chance as this was not only my moment to shine but to also have a future team of sales reps working to get me booked for future speaking engagements, which was considered a huge win for my speaking career.

That day I took the stage and greeted the audience. About ten minutes into my presentation an unfamiliar feeling washed over me. At first I couldn't identify the feeling and just chalked it up to nerves. I kept going with my talk, but the feeling got stronger. Ten more minutes went by and the feeling became clearer; my intuition was screaming at me to change the course of my speech.

As I spoke my thoughts were wrestling inside me, I was thinking should I or shouldn't I? I was trying to decipher if my psyche was sending me on the greatest sabotage mission of my career or if I should follow my intuition and change my speech. Here I was totally prepared and right in the midst of delivering an incredible keynote, yet I wanted to shift gears and go in a different direction.

Keep in mind, my drive for perfection in everything I do is very high so this decision left me feeling incredibly uncomfortable. I had no idea how the presentation would be received or even how I would find the words to deliver it. It was not the first time I had ever put myself into a position of voluntary discomfort, but it was the first I had ever done it in front of an audience.

Imagine my nerves and my own surprise as I set down my slide advancer and left my carefully choreographed presentation to share an entirely different one. My voice shook slightly, at first, only to be matched by my shaking hands, as I took off in a completely unprepared and new direction with the audience that day. I left my comfort zone and boldly committed to following my gut instinct even in the midst of this unexpected place of feeling uncomfortable. What ensued was one of the most engaging keynotes I had given to date.

Normally a speaker can measure their performance by a standing ovation, number of books sold, or the number of people wanting to connect after an event is over. On that day, I was shocked. To date, I had usually had no more than 10 people reach out to me after a keynote but on this day I had about 60 people lined up wanting to talk and share how my presentation had touched their hearts and situations. In my own vulnerability and place of discomfort, I was able to resonate and connect with the audience.

I often wonder how life would have stayed the same if I hadn't followed my intuition that day. I would have delivered my carefully prepared and precisely choreographed keynote speech and have no doubt it would have been well received. However, because I was willing to be bold and stretch even when I didn't clearly see why and I could not calculate the outcome with any precision, I delivered a keynote that day that was magical. I was not only able to inspire the audience and create raving fans with my speaker's bureau, but I also experienced tremendous personal growth that day.

Most speakers have a system in how they like to communicate and that day I stepped out of the way I normally presented my material. This was a pivotal point for me in reaching the next level of refinement of my speaking and leadership skills. I felt empowered as I allowed myself to go off script.

There is something to be said for being prepared. I will never tell you to enter into any professional engagement unprepared, but there is also something to be said for being open to possibilities. I learned a great deal about myself that day. I saw a side of me that I hadn't seen before, one that could command an audience by being authentic and non-scripted.

By pushing through my fears of letting go of complete control, I was able to nurture skills that actually enabled me to touch the audience deeper than I had ever been able to do before. I was bold and through doing that, I achieved bolder results, not only for myself, but also for those I was leading that day.

VOLUNTARY DISCOMFORT

The feeling of personal and professional growth I had that day was tremendous. Even more important was the realization that if I wanted to achieve more awesome results, I had to change how I did things. I recognized that I had to push myself to stretch and feel uncomfortable more often.

To achieve the level of awesome I wanted for my life, I had to extend beyond my current safety perimeters and be okay with the idea that, at times, I will be uncomfortable and maybe even afraid. I learned through my speaking experience that day that in my uncertainty and discomfort I would grow and reach a potential that I never had before or had not even thought possible. Quite frankly, it wasn't possible before because I wasn't willing to go through the discomfort required to grow and learn.

The great news in all of this is that as the famed American author Oliver Wendell Holmes says, "Man's mind, once stretched by a new idea, never regains its original dimensions."

Once your mind has been stretched with learning and experiences there is no going back to its previous shape. The discomfort you will feel in the stretching and the growing will be temporary, but through the result of that experience, you will change positively. When faced with the situation again, the discomfort will be replaced by confidence and the lasting wisdom that comes from experience. As your confidence grows it will become easier for you to navigate situations and consider new ways of doing things.

THE TIME IS NOW

The best time to press through fear and experience something new that might be out of your comfort zone is now. Go the extra mile, push your limits, see if you can see a better solution (not just what might feel comfortable) and really challenge yourself in your thinking, in your capabilities, and in your knowledge

Chapter 9

Many of us are afraid to jump out of our comfort zone and allow ourselves to be uncomfortable. The problem with that is that people usually don't make changes unless they are uncomfortable in some way. Without any discomfort, there is no change; without any change, there is no growth, and without growth, it will be impossible for you to reach your awesome.

For example, even when you are sitting in a chair, as long as you are comfortable you won't shift positions, you will stay in the same old spot. Only as you are sitting and feel pain somewhere or perhaps your leg falls asleep will you change your position to search for comfort again. The same goes for life. You can choose to be complacent and stay in the same place with your life, career or relationships and be totally fine with it.

I'm suggesting to shift your position and identify if there is an opportunity to own your awesome in a much bigger way. You need to be willing to commit to being uncomfortable and make decisions that require new growth. Being uncomfortable is how you are going to change, grow and make progress, but most importantly how you are going to reach and own your awesome.

SERVE OTHERS

The decision that day to change the direction of my keynote address was made out of a desire and intuition to serve someone else. I wanted to serve the audience in the best way I could and for some reason my internal compass led me to completely go off script. Often times it is easier to show bold courage by making a difference through serving others. It is easier to speak up and advocate for someone else than it is to do it for ourselves. The reason for this is our own self-worth, which we will get into more later. But for our purposes right now, all we need is the understanding that it is easier to serve others than ourselves.

> The problem with that is that people usually don't make changes unless they are uncomfortable in some way.

If you find it difficult at first to stretch and find a voice for yourself then you can ease into it and find ways to be of service to others. Find ways to step outside your comfort zone and see extraordinary opportunities in ordinary daily activities. Take each situation and consider how you can turn it around and make an extraordinary impact for someone else.

Soon it will become second nature and will be so easy for you to step out and serve others that the idea of being uncomfortable won't matter anymore. Some examples of ways of serving others are recognizing their efforts, championing their needs, speaking up for those who can't speak for themselves, showing compassion to their situation and creating a community of support for their cause. There are numerous ways to be bold and stretch yourself when it comes to the needs of others.

I remember one day entering a bank to make a deposit. It was like any other normal end of the month bank visit with a long line-up of people eager to get their banking done and get out to enjoy their weekend. There was at least 30 people in the line-up when I arrived. It was so long it seemed like it would take forever to get through to the front.

We were a typical queue in the sense that everyone was in their own little world. Nobody talked to each other because our minds were preoccupied with other things. The common thread was that we were all resigned to have to wait in this long line to do some simple banking.

As I stood there I did what every other person does when they are in a line, which was to look down or be entertained with my phone. It seemed like hours but it was finally my turn. The bank teller was a lovely, sweet and animated woman in her mid-50s. She didn't make me feel pressed or a bother in her constant line-up of the day; she actually made me feel like I was her chosen customer. She gave me the impression she was going to take as long as I needed in order to help me that day. I felt like a million dollars and that my bank business was important.

Even though I could feel the pressure of the eyes of the other bank clients willing me to hurry up, the teller proceeded to do my deposit and answer a few questions I had about a discrepancy on my account. She made me feel like I was the only customer who mattered and she had time for me. I was extremely appreciative of her time and patience after my long week. For most it would have been an ordinary moment in the day, but the teller made me feel important.

I suddenly felt bold and wanted to do for her the same thing she had done for me. I laugh to myself to this day as I recall the shocked look on the faces of everyone in the bank as I boldly turned around and said in my best announcer voice, "Excuse me". Louder still. "Excuse me." I said. "May I have everyone's attention please?"

At that moment, my teller looked perplexed. I went on to say "It is my honor to nominate Claudia as employee of the day today. She just gave me the best customer service and I would like to ask everyone to give Claudia a round of applause." I took a seemingly ordinary moment and turned it into something extraordinary for someone else. Was I feeling a bit of discomfort? You bet I was!

What happened next was even beyond what I expected. The other customers in line suddenly realized they were called to action and started clapping, their eyes fixated on Claudia. There was a chain reaction as the other 20 bank staff realized all of these people were clapping and smiling for one of their own. Their shoulders went back, big smiles erupted on their faces, and it was like the light switch was turned on.

I looked around the room at the results of pushing myself to step into a short term voluntary moment of discomfort, and I was pleased with the result. The bank staff all were now giving direct eye contact to their customers and the waiting customers were talking with each another, laughing and smiling about what just happened. In one instance of bold courage, it awakened a connection in a community. In this situation, it was the bank. The manager was in awe and we later talked about the lasting effects of validating her employee in that way and what it did to the morale of the individual, the team and the overall culture at the bank.

I didn't plan that day to do something bold. It was honestly a spur of the moment crazy decision that I took action on. However, upon reflection of the outcome of stretching out of my comfort zone, it got me thinking. In finding the awesome in others it helped me find the awesome in me as well. By taking that risk, I rediscovered what exhilaration felt like again.

PART 3
A CASE CALLED WORTHY

CHAPTER 10
FREEDOM THROUGH FAILING

I never expected that stretching out of my comfort zone a little would result in such exhilaration and leave me hungry for more, but it did. I craved more of that awesome feeling and looked for ways in all aspects of my life that I could create more opportunity to step out of my comfort zone and into bold courage.

As I took stock of my thoughts and beliefs I realized that although I had let go of the past I also needed to recognize how I was dealing with the present. I needed to recognize some serious truths about how I was coping and seeing life at the time.

Without even realizing it, I was on edge and living in a reactive state, ready to solve the next big problem that came my way.

Have you ever heard the phrase, "if it ain't broke, don't fix it?" I was guilty of violating that rule all the time. I would literally look for things that could possibly go wrong and try and find solutions for them even before they occurred and then simply wait for the moment to spring into action. Let me be the one to tell you that if you haven't lived this way yourself, it is exhausting and it never ends.

Because of that mindset there was a definite disconnect from how I was living to the mind frame in which I wanted to live. Where I wanted to live was a place of hope, joy and positivity, but that is tremendously hard to do when you are busy preparing for the next big failure.

I realized I was prevented from getting there because I was afraid of not being perfect all the time and failing. This was a huge realization. That recognition alone had a major impact on my ability to boldly stride forward towards owning my awesome.

From that day on I challenged my thinking of what failure meant to me. I had to let go of my feelings of inadequacy and not being perfect and recognize that things are not always going to go 100 percent as I hope and that it was fine. I had to be vulnerable and allow myself to be unsure of possible outcomes in order to allow myself to grow.

At the same time I recognized that the process of owning my awesome required me to have bold courage, including stretching out of my comfort zone and having the occasional misstep along the way.

My view of failure at the time was defined as any time I didn't achieve perfection or had a slip-up of some sort, no matter how miniscule. With me there was no level of failure. Anything less than perfect was all one level, which was catastrophic. I realized that somehow for more than 40 years, I connected my self-worth to what others thought and rather than finding peace in my decisions, I found myself in constant need of validation and recognition from the outside.

Failure was a place of high drama in my life and a sore spot where in some way there was evidence that I had toiled, invested time, energy, emotions and finances aiming for the "prize" and proof that I never quite succeeded.

In the wake of a failure I would judge that I didn't quite make the mark, that I wasn't good enough and I would find myself lost and seemingly abandoned in the abyss of my other lost ideas. What I didn't recognize at that time was that my worth and value do not come from my failures but rather from the act of trying.

I quickly realized that the only way I could test what failure really should have meant to me was to become more daring in how I approached new opportunities. I gave myself permission to use all my experiences as a place of learning and growth rather than a place of judgment.

> Worth and value do not come from my failures but rather from the act of trying.

When I first started reflecting on past failures in my own life, I realized there were many efforts along the way and some calculated risks that I would categorize as failures. There were ideas or goals that I set out to conquer that never seemed to come to fruition. Instead they were cast aside and thrown into a pit of lost ideas, bad decisions and just plain stupid moves.

I know there are numerous books that talk about failure being a great thing but the act of failing doesn't feel good to anyone. I decided to change my thinking on that subject. Instead of focusing on the act of failing, I decided to focus on the gifts that come out of the "journey" through failing.

In the case of bold courage, failure along the way is a reality, a certainty and something you must recognize as inevitable. How you learn to deal with it, learn from it and grow from it makes all the difference in owning your awesome. You need to recognize that you will make mistakes, you will have setbacks, and things will still turn out fine.

> I gave myself permission to use all my experiences as a place of learning and growth rather than a place of judgment.

RECOGNIZED FOR GOOD WORK

Everyone loves to be recognized for good work. It doesn't matter your age, gender or socioeconomic status; the fact is, everyone likes recognition. It is a pleasure and a nice bonus when we get recognition from others. However, the most important recognition comes from within ourselves. We don't often give ourselves enough credit for the work we do and the attempts we make.

Make recognizing what is amazing about you a priority. Give yourself a break and stop being so critical with unrealistic expectations. Recognize that although you might be afraid, there is no reason to get upset by any perceived missteps. Whether the day was perfect or not it can still be seen as a success, but it has to start with your attitude. You can actually have fun by looking at your failures as great learning experiences and as a springboard to what you will do differently next time.

Your journey to bold courage will be marred with failures. Being ready to recognize their significance is key to growth. When you do that you will know what to do differently next time. Your journey is a collection of steps. It isn't one decision nor is it defined by one act; it is the sum of everything.

There will be many days that go smoothly and others when things creep up and seem like chaos has struck again and you take a step backwards in your progress. To keep yourself on track, put things in perspective and recognize that you have the power to change how the story of your journey ends. It doesn't end simply because you have a bad day or even a bad week. You have the power to change that and put your thoughts and feelings into the right proportion within the grand scale of things.

Remind yourself that your bold courage journey to owning your awesome is not linear art, but it is more of an abstract creation. It isn't a simple math equation where every day you add a+b+c=d. Sometimes external conditions and unexpected circumstances can throw the balance off of the equation, but you still can get to "d."

Remember you cannot control the world, even though you may want to. You can only control yourself and how you react to situations. If you can react with wisdom and confidence in knowing that setbacks are only temporary learning curves, you will feel better and stronger.

Through my reflection of how I was treating failure, I found something precious and that was freedom. I realized that there is freedom in failing because it allows me to see things more clearly and learn and there is nothing more freeing than getting real with myself. It also made me aware that when I thought things were falling apart, often they were actually falling into place.

On your journey to owning your awesome, it is imperative that you recognize that failure is okay.

RECOGNITION FROM OTHERS

Showing praise and learning to appreciate and recognize the efforts of others should become a part of your boldness strategy. In turn they will often become cheerleaders for you and support your efforts along the way.

I've been fortunate in my life and have had many cheerleaders in my corner who I can always count on to help me feel supported, loved and recognized as I worked at making important and lasting changes to my life. Although the internal recognition I gave myself was a foundation, it also made the journey easier to have people around me who could remind me of the positives when I forgot or got burdened by the events of the day.

The road to owning your awesome can sometimes feel like a lonely one, but it doesn't have to be. Look around you and see how people contribute to your life. There will be those who are cheerleaders and willing to lend a hand and lift you up and dust you off when everything seems uphill and then there are those who spray dirt in your face as you fall. Choose your people wisely!

Find more of those people who are willing to share and be generous with their journey and with their willingness to remind you of your awesome on those days when your own vision is cloudy. For me, this has made a huge difference in the speed with which I can recover from a setback. It is a great feeling to be able to be vulnerable and share my challenges, and also to share my wins. Celebrating is a big motivator during times of change. The more people you get to celebrate, the better because the celebrations are that much sweeter when experienced with those who understand the process.

PART 3
A CASE CALLED WORTHY

CHAPTER 11
EMBRACING CHAOS

If we could go shopping for chaos in a store, it would be kept in a box with a childproof label way up on the tallest shelf with a big glaring warning label saying "CHAOS – warning - contents under pressure", "CHAOS – warning - may explode if heated" or even "CHAOS – open with caution, this spreads."

There are many sources of chaos and many different types of chaos that turn a perfectly peaceful time into complete insanity. Certainly throughout people's lives chaos has created havoc and been a source for upset and drama at least once and usually many times. The one thing I know for sure about chaos is that it often hits without any warning.

If we let it, chaos will push us off our intended direction and leave us confused and unsure of what to do next. It is like a tornado that rips through a town with ferocious winds leaving anything in its path in ruins. The winds scoop up the unsuspecting victim, spinning them in circles until they are so dizzy they can't focus and then spitting them out in an unfamiliar place. Some towns and structures survive wind and chaos and others don't and succumb to the spin.

The fact that some people survive chaos and others crumble in its wake got me thinking about why that might be. No matter the reason for the chaos, the result is almost always the same; some people are left unharmed and others are deeply affected by the instability that chaos can give. I have decided that the outcome of chaos and the ease of survival for a person experiencing it can be forecasted by looking at how they react when the disruption hits.

With as many unique personalities as there are in the world, it is not surprising that there are a number of different and unique reactions people have when they experience chaos. I have seen many of my clients experience personal and professional chaos over the years of my career and the reactions vary from mild to intense in nature. It is interesting to note that although the specifics of reaction to chaos will vary, there are common overarching themes of response. These are valuable to know when we are assessing the likelihood of survival through chaos.

Some people who face chaos will become overwhelmed and incapacitated. They basically freeze up, unable to move or make decisions. Other people will give way to panic and act irrationally and do things they normally wouldn't. There are those who simply become overwhelmed with emotion and fear of impending doom.

None of these reactions make it easy to soar through chaos unscathed. These kind of reactions are just that – reactions, meaning you are living in a reactive state in which you roll with the punches and never have more of a plan than what is right in front of you.

The truth is that we can all get swept up in the daily chaos of life, but it is then that we need to be calm. Chaos is a combination of what you create and what you allow. Those individuals who survive chaos are those people who can remain grounded and keep stillness inside them when everyone else is losing their cool.

Great leaders provide a compass and a sense of direction to themselves and to all those around them in the midst of the chaos. It's almost like they hold

> Chaos is a combination of what you create and what you allow.

Chapter 11

the magic compass and ensure that any decisions that are made are consistent and aligned with their previously defined vision, values and guidelines. As you journey to owning your awesome with bold courage you will be required to do the same.

You will need to become the leader of your own life and always carry your own compass. The good news is that because you have previously defined your awesome (your desired state), it makes it much easier to remain calm and have clarity while your environment seems to spin out of control. When you are prepared you become proactive and can put things into perspective more easily and recognize and make decisions. You already know where you want to go and how you want to live your life and own your awesome; determining that was the tough part! Just like we talked about in Chapter 6 when you learned about being committed and finding relevance in actions and decisions, you will do the same when chaos strikes.

You need to decipher what has relevance to your journey and what doesn't. Remember, chaos is a combination of what you create and what you allow. If you allow clutter and anxiety to enter your realm that is what you will live. However, if you use your bold courage and kick the useless clutter and anxiety to the curb as quickly as it entered, the chaos can be swiftly dissolved.

Here are a few things to remember when chaos strikes. Stay calm and do not allow panic to overtake rational thinking. Rational thinking will enable you to make decision with confidence and clarity rather than emotion. Take stock and really reflect on what is happening around you and what is being presented before you. Ask yourself if the chaos is even yours or does it have to do with someone else and thus is not something for you to take on.

We often get caught up in other people's chaos and then get bogged down even when it was never ours to assume. If it isn't yours, remove yourself from it. If it is yours, get clear on what needs attention and what needs kicking to the curb. Anything that doesn't further your desire to own your awesome gets kicked out. Examine every area of chaos that is swirling around you and either deal with it or cast it out.

Lastly, commit to doing your best. Not every decision and situation will be perfect, but that's part of the journey and it is all right to make mistakes.

BEAUTY IN DISARRAY

So far we have looked at the negative side of chaos, but there is also beauty to be found in the midst of disarray. Sometimes you can find opportunity in places you would not have seen if chaos hadn't struck you. You would have missed opportunities.

As you use your compass to navigate through chaos, be open to seeing if there is a detour along the way or a better way. Find something of value that matches your direction of awesome and when you see it, grab it.

A few years ago my business partner and I flew into Toronto for three full days of business meetings. We had a lot to do in the few days we were there so we packed our schedule tight with back-to-back meetings and events. By some strange course of events three of our most important meetings were cancelled on our last day. We were counting on these meetings and had high hopes for the outcome of each so we were greatly disappointed.

Due to the cancellations what first appeared to be a smart investment of time, energy and money now looked to be a colossal waste of it all. Our plan was ruined as three of our largest meetings were cancelled (out of our control) and now our strategic plan was in danger of failing because we couldn't meet the timelines we thought we would have been able to work within.

Rather than panic, we decided to take a walk and get a quick breath of fresh air. We were staying in downtown Toronto so as we left our hotel one of the first things that could be seen was the CN Tower. As my business partner turned to look up at the Tower, she blurted out that we should do the CN Tower Edgewalk that afternoon. I surprised myself as I readily agreed, despite the chaos I was feeling in my business that day, not to mention my fear of heights!

The CN Tower is one of the world's tallest structures and the Edgewalk requires you to walk around the circumference of the tower outside in the elements, 116 stories above the ground, attached to two rappel lines, walking on a four foot metal mesh walkway with no safety railings! Be still my heart! I couldn't believe I had just agreed to do that! What was I thinking?

After inquiring about availability with registration at the Edgewalk check- in, we were all set! Our reservation was in about an hour which gave us just enough time to grab a quick bite to eat and get excited for what we were about to do. Soon enough it was our time to prepare for the walk!

We signed several pieces of paper basically indicating we wouldn't hold them responsible if something went wrong and we plunged to our deaths, a health questionnaire, removed all of our jewelry, emptied pockets, pulled our hair back, passed a breathalyzer test and then we were suited up with the proper jumpsuit and body harness.

The anticipation was building and I was getting extremely anxious, I could feel my breathing start to speed up and my heart race. I was sweating at the thought of what we were about to do.

We finished suiting up and waited for our names to be called for our turn. The big moment arrived – the one we had been anticipating where we would leave the safety of the tower and step out onto the narrow platform gazing out over the skyscrapers and Lake Ontario far below.

It was terrifying and I held my rappel line with white knuckles. I remember my feet shuffling forward moving me outside. Everything was flashing through my mind, including the thought that we were crazy for doing this. I questioned who would voluntarily sign themselves up for an experience that would compel them to go through security, sign numerous forms, pass a breathalyzer and make themselves completely vulnerable all in the name of having a challenge?

Everything felt chaotic. Fear was rampant just being out on the ledge. We were pinned against the side of the Tower, but our guide got us lined up and prepared for the next stage of our adventure, which was to press our fear limits even further.

The adventure included several challenges as we made our way around the edge. The first exercise was to simply unglue ourselves from the side of the building and step out towards the edge of the platform and hang the front two inches of our toes over the edge, standing there with nothing to hold onto.

I was the lucky one chosen to go first. I shuffled my feet slowly towards the edge with every fiber of my body telling me not to. When you are in chaos, your body can go into a fight or flight mode. Mine was definitely in flight mode, but I mentally calmed myself and pushed on. Due to my fear, I couldn't look down and actually see where my feet were so I had to keep asking if I was there yet. I made it to the edge and looked around at what was one of the most spectacular views I have ever seen.

The second challenge was to allow our harness to take our weight and back our bodies out over the edge of the platform in midair, feet on the outside edge of the platform, arms outstretched and knees locked with our body suspended over the city. We were supposed to create a pike position with our bodies posed over the ground below.

I was again chosen to go first. I felt a little more confident as I made my way into this position. I found myself out over the edge before I knew it and my feelings of chaos and fear were replaced by pride and excitement, I was grinning ear to ear and everyone cheered me on. Joy and accomplishment spread across my face and a feeling of complete

Chapter 11

exhilaration and freedom as the wind blew through my hair and I threw my arms out to experience the thrill.

I owned that moment and found beauty in my chaos, one that from that day on I would hunger for again and again.

The next challenge had everyone uneasy. It was clearly the big finale and was the exact opposite to the previous action. We were supposed to stand about one and a half feet from the edge of the platform and drop our rope, allowing it to support our shoulders as our bodies fell out horizontal to the ground with nothing but air and skyscrapers below! We were supposed to rest our chests on our rope and allow the rope to take the weight of our bodies as we were suspended high above Toronto.

I wasn't first this time; my business partner was. I was rather happy about that. The guide encouraged her to move forward as she had flown through the other challenges with ease and we all thought this one would be no different. But it was different this time as she made several attempts to let go and allow her body to suspend forward to no avail. I could see on her face the internal chaos she was fighting. It was only minutes, but later she told me it felt like hours as she tried to find calm and complete the task.

I don't know where this came from -- somewhere deep inside of me I guess -- but suddenly watching my friend struggle I stepped forward with complete clarity and I asked her if she wanted to do it together. We would both go at the same time, and let go at the same time. That was all she needed and we stepped forward and hung face down off the edge of one of the world's tallest buildings with our hands outstretched and free at the complete mercy of a rope that we trusted to hold our weight.

That day I was reminded that I held a compass as a leader and had the ability to turn chaos into calm not only for myself, but also for my team.

We left the Tower that day more confident as individuals and as a team. We were grateful we made the decision to say yes. For me, I had felt my pulse race and anxiety try and take over that day, yet instead I found my bold courage and faced the fear, kicked chaos to the curb and accepted joy, exhilaration and calm and it felt wonderful.

From that experience, I challenged my thinking of what embracing chaos would mean for me going forward. I now see it differently and spend more time enjoying the thrill of the ride, willing to live in uncertain moments with my pulse racing and heart pounding.

Opportunity for great growth lies in chaos, and now when I feel that familiar rush of chaos I know that I will withstand the pressure as my compass is set in the right direction. It keeps me on track and focused on what is important and open to what I can learn. You will also learn to do the same as you journey with bold courage to find and own your awesome.

PART 3

A CASE CALLED WORTHY

CHAPTER 12

WHEN THE STAKES GET HIGH

It's almost here, that big moment you've been waiting for. Your stomach is in knots and everything from finance, hope and sweat is on the line. Your heart is beating heavily as you will yourself to slow down and take in large gulps of air in an effort not to hyperventilate.

You'd think I was talking about the moment right before you make a huge company-wide presentation, or being on the edge of finding a cure for cancer, or maybe even launching into outer space. But I'm not talking about any of that.

I'm talking about every day stress when the stakes get high. However, the feelings I described can be real and just as terrifying as if I had been talking about shooting off into space. Feelings of fear are real and can often make you feel as though there is a lot on the line, and sometimes there is. You've worked hard, expended a lot of time and resources and you are heavily invested in your endeavor. You have set the bar high, with expectations focused on successful outcomes. The question to ask yourself is: do you have the courage to get there?

The effects of courage in relation to risk have a powerful impact. Courage is what moves competitors into the winner's circle, that proverbial place of status that highlights the accomplishments and affirms to the individual that persistence and hard work pay off. It takes courage to take risks. Risk, if approached in the correct fashion, becomes a core part of your winning game plan to own your awesome. The process of learning to manage risk balanced with courage at a tolerable level for you is yours to discover.

You aren't alone in that discovery process. I can remember walking out onto a stage for a crucial presentation many years ago, trying to hide the fact that I was fearful and praying that I didn't faint in front of a few hundred spectators. I was so disappointed in myself at that moment for feeling so miserable, vulnerable and teetering on the edge of feeling humiliated and embarrassed. I was so worried that I wasn't good enough and that I couldn't stand on my own laurels. That day, my uncertainly and disbelief in myself resulted not just in a poor presentation, it was a colossal bomb.

That experience happened at the same time I was attempting to decipher my way through the very risky technology company I had started. The risk and emotional burden was very high on all fronts. The addition of this company to my already full career took a tremendous amount of time, energy, focus and finances away from my already busy life. The financial risk was huge, so much so that I had invested most of my retirement nest egg and my savings account. I did so willingly as I believed the financial probability of a large return was high.

My desire was also high to create a solution that would make a difference in the lives of many, and also provide a nice financial gain for my family. At every turn risk was apparent and I often felt far outside my comfort zone as I was aware of the impact it would have to lose my investment.

After I made the decision to launch this new venture, I felt the risk and the extreme responsibility for all involved. I recognized that while I knew what my own subject matter expertise was, I wasn't that familiar with the technology sector as a whole. I knew I needed to become more familiar with the commonly used verbiage and industry speak, not to mention the overall landscape of what it takes to be successful in such a fast-paced industry. What I did know is that in life, nothing trumps wisdom. So learning the ropes was the first point of focus for me. I wanted to become well versed to be able to make informed decisions along the way.

INFORMATION OVERLOAD

During this time of intensive learning, I felt I was very fortunate to meet numerous people who were considered to be superstars within the field. Even though they didn't have my experience, I believed that their perspective would be extremely helpful for me to make informed decisions more easily.

To make up for what I felt were my shortcomings in this sector, I built my own advisory group of mentors, who shared their stories, ideas and knowledge with me regularly. We had many meetings with conversations surrounding what was the best approach, smartest marketing positioning and the most recommended people to hire. Even though it was technology specific knowledge I was seeking, we literally spoke of every aspect of my business, even areas where I was already successfully running it. At that point I was already a multi award winning entrepreneur and bestselling author, but I allowed them to offer their input anyway.

Information came from so many directions it felt like a sky of shooting stars flashing through the air and then landing on my head. All of those ideas and suggestions would have been ideal had all the advice been consistent, aligned, and related to the issue I was trying to solve. However, the advice varied widely and often conflicted directly with other advisors, with each one holding fast to their ideas, judgments or suggestions on how I should run my business. They each stressed the risk of my impending failure if I chose the other's advice and direction. My stomach was in knots most of the time.

Because of this, unbeknownst to me at the time, something was shifting in me. What I had first thought as a smart strategy for growing my business was actually deeply hampering my success. I thought I could skip some steps and find the easy button by relying on the knowledge of those around me. I engaged in so many conversations with various people with differing opinions that my fear rose to an all-time high.

I was polarized to make decisions due to my fear of failure and constantly second-guessed my own judgments. I was no longer the CEO of my vision but had elevated about ten others to the CEO status. I relied on their differing opinions and ideas to make decisions for my company.

It created absolute chaos and confusion in my world. I didn't feel or act like the visionary or success story I had long ago proved I was. Now when I look back on that time, I recognize that I had given away my power to all the others that I assumed knew more than me. In the process I lost my confidence and my vision for the future. I was so cluttered with everyone else's ideas and rationale that I lost my own ability to function effectively and because of that I started to stumble.

As I progressed through the season of building the technology company, I learned a valuable lesson; mentors are a dime a dozen. Everyone has an opinion and most feel that their way is best and in many instances the only way. This was so confusing to me as I tried to decipher what was the best way to proceed through my journey.

Being the people pleaser that I am, I got caught up in the drama of making decisions and trying to please others without making any use of my own experience and knowledge or even considering what I wanted. Decisions became harder as I relied on everyone else's knowledge, assuming their understanding was better than mine.

The danger of that, apart from losing confidence in my own abilities and experience as a successful businesswoman, was the sheer time it started to take me to make decisions in a very competitive, fast-paced industry. I felt I had to rush around and check with about a dozen people to make sure they thought it was a good choice. Any time a crossroads would arise I could no longer make a decision on my own.

I recognized that it was not clarity I received from all of this mentoring, but quite the opposite. By trying to skip ahead with my own learning and relying on everyone else's knowledge I actually forgot my own strengths and experiences that had brought me success in my other companies. The results were that I was less confident and actually less able than I had been in a long time.

I had contracted what I now term as "mentor fatigue." I asked too many people their opinion and in effect I became over stimulated with too much information. Mentor fatigue is real and often times dangerous to your progress. When you are yearning for results as the stakes get higher and your perceived level of risk peaks, the natural tendency is to look outside yourself to seek answers. I am living testimony that that isn't always the case.

When I stopped holding everyone else's opinions higher than my own it reignited some belief in myself. I recognized that I had the power to succeed and envision the life I desired. I was also able to make smart decisions and start taking action again without the need to consult anyone.

I don't want to give you the wrong impression about seeking out a mentor; I definitely encourage you to continue to seek answers and wisdom from others. But this whole experience reframed my thinking about what mentorship and advice means. Getting mentorship is a critical part of learning and expanding your knowledge base as individuals and as business people, but it is not meant to replace what you already know. Mentorship is meant to enhance your own knowledge, not replace it.

The power of owning your awesome is anchored in the ability to lead your vision well. The operative word is "your" vision, as it is your perspective on how your life should be lived and what actions you believe will affect positive change, growth or impact your long term success.

The journey to owning your awesome will always require bold courage to ask for advice and mentorship. The trick is to make sure you are asking for the right information from the right people. Make sure they truly have the knowledge and experience you are looking for. Anyone can say they are an expert at something but check into whether they have realized success and growth in the areas at which you aspire to become better. Or is their expertise just their own ego and surface marketing jargon designed to make them look good?

> Mentorship is meant to enhance your own knowledge, not replace it.

Be diligent with these relationships and do your homework to feel confident and be able to trust that your mentors know what they are talking about and are not just giving off the cuff advice.

Once you find the right mentors, trust them and forget the need to continually validate their input with several other people as you look for the same answers to the same questions. I lost almost two years of business growth by listening and heeding advice that did not work well or make sense. This caused me to get off track and lose momentum. The process of winning involves knowing when to take useful information and pivot where you need to in order to gain success. I have now learned when and how I take information in and how to use the information more wisely.

I appreciate and recognize the learning that mentor fatigue brought into my life. It completely changed the way I see and build relationships when it comes to successful mentorship. The goal of these relationships should be very specific and focused on pulling ideas and knowledge from mentors that make sense and to apply or discuss them in context to your vision.

In the end, your vision should be the final factor in whether you implement any advice and if it connects to you as the leader. As visionaries of our own awesome, each one of us brings our own personality and style to the table and we should pair it with a uniquely crafted course of action that makes sense to us.

As you forge ahead, remain true to yourself and avoid getting lost in mentor fatigue. As a result of my experience, today I am very careful how I provide mentorship to people. I choose to mentor only if I feel I have relevance to offer to those seeking my help. Mentoring still keeps me busy.

A number of years ago I was inducted into Canada's Top Ten Mentor Rock Stars by Start Up Canada, yet I am careful to only offer my advice on subjects in which I truly have knowledge and experience. I still remind the mentees that they have wisdom within themselves and to check it often.

Mentoring can be a wonderful experience for both sides as it can foster inspiration, clarity of vision and affirm potential. It can also challenge you to take risks and say yes or to slow down and be more cautious.

The benefits are clearly valuable, but so are the downfalls if you rely on mentors too much. Give yourself some grace and credit as you journey to owning your awesome. Keep faith and trust in your abilities even when the stakes get high and the risk is great. Don't allow fear to cloud what you already know. Instead, allow yourself the courage to admit what you don't know and seek help in those areas. . Rely on yourself in those areas that you do know. Everything will be fine.

PART 3
A CASE CALLED WORTHY

CHAPTER 13
JUST ONE THING

Almost everyone has heard of the starfish story. It is one of my favorite stories of triumph. It's the tale of a young boy on a beach where thousands of starfish have been left behind by the tide and are at risk of dying in the hot sun.

If you have ever spent any time by the ocean you know that the tide often carries sea creatures to the shore, leaving them with limited time to get out of the hot sun and back to the safety of the water before it's too late.

In the starfish story there is a little boy on the beach who finds a large number of starfish that need to get back to the water before they bake in the sun. An old man sits by watching with interest in what the young boy is doing. The job seems endless and impossible to the old man watching the boy from afar.

The man walks over to the boy in an effort to tell him not to waste his time as he can't possibly save all those starfish before they die. The boy nods his head and pointedly replies as he tosses one more starfish into the safety of the water that he made a difference to that one.

The boy saw the impact he could make even in the small steps and celebrated being able to make a difference. He had gratitude and was satisfied with his effort to save each starfish that he could. He didn't spend his time thinking mournful thoughts about what he couldn't do and what he couldn't achieve. He took action and saved as many starfish as he could that day. He regarded every returned starfish as a victory and claimed the joy that came with each successful step.

A lot can be learned from the power of that short story. There is much wisdom that we can use as a reminder to ourselves on the journey to owning our awesome. We don't need to make grandiose acts to make a difference and it is often the small everyday acts that make the biggest difference.

We all have the power to make a difference in our own lives and those that are directly around us. The knowledge that each one of us has the capacity to make that difference is a gift. It is a gift that has taken me years to fully understand. With my realization of that gift I gained, through the strength of my visions, the power to shape my future. You have the same power to shape your future exactly how you want it.

The challenge becomes easier if we ready ourselves like the boy in the story. We need to celebrate our wins more often, even if those wins seem small. When we embrace gratitude for what we have, it is easier to be satisfied with our effort and results. When we are satisfied with our effort and results, we become more productive. There's that interesting pattern again!

Gratitude has an amazing power in your life if you allow it. Gratitude is a lifestyle choice that goes hand in hand with bold courage and owning your awesome. It is the one thing without a doubt that can keep you motivated, healthier and happier.

Health studies show that those expressing gratitude brings many benefits. A 2008 study by psychologist Alex Wood published in the *Journal of research in Personality* shows grateful people are less inclined to suffer from depression. A 2012 study in the journal *Personality and Individual Differences* revealed people who practice gratitude take better care of themselves, including exercising and having regular checkups. They even sleep better, according to a 2011 study published in the peer-reviewed journal *Applied Psychology: Health and Well-Being.*

All of these benefits will help you protect yourself in building a resiliency to any challenges you will encounter as you make changes in your life.

It is easy to be grateful in moments of abundance and prosperity, when everything is going well and you are on the top of your game. Where the human spirit is tried is in showing gratitude in those times considered more challenging in life.

For example, when things are going our way, we are in a good mood, we are happy, the sun may be shining, our future looks bright and gratitude seems to exude from our very pores. We become thankful and excited about what is next to come. In times of challenge and disruption when things seem darker and rougher, it is harder to be thankful.

For example, something may not have gone your way. You may have been overlooked for a promotion, missed an opportunity, or lost a big client. That is the exact time when you need gratitude the most. Gratitude sets the stage for keeping you in a calmer and more focused state of mind.

Your journey to owning your awesome is not a race. The small steps along the journey are not only a reality, but are an essential and critical part of the process. In today's instant society, we typically want success and we want it now. That is normal and completely understandable, albeit in this instance also completely unrealistic. Confidence and contentment is found in being aware and learning to appreciate every single step of your journey.

> Gratitude sets the stage for keeping you in a calmer and more focused state of mind.

Give yourself the credit you deserve for the hard work you are putting in and celebrate those milestones of accomplishment. Living intentionally requires each step to be focused and specific as you commit to take action to owning your awesome.

When you add up all of the little steps you make, they create a powerful force that is unstoppable. It may seem slow to get your proverbial vehicle moving, but once it starts it moves like a steamroller going down a hill. The steamroller is powerful and is able to move any obstacle that comes into its path. Think of your small steps like the steamroller. Nothing is a match for the strength of your many small steps when they are bound together by time and gratitude.

The boy on the beach was happy and celebrated his small steps of saving one starfish at a time. What is memorable about that story is that over time he may well have saved thousands of starfish by small steps each day. In this type of situation, our natural tendency might be to call anything less than saving all of the starfish that day a failure. In changing perspective to think like the little boy, you can instead take a personal stand and commit to make a difference. Surrender yourself to what you cannot control, take action on what you can control, and celebrate the rest.

> Nothing is a match for the strength of your many small steps when they are bound together by time and gratitude.

WISDOM FROM SMALL STEPS

Wisdom often comes from the understanding of how experiences impact your life. It is through what happens to us and our responses to it that we learn and understand and grow with small steps, not giant leaps.

Sometimes we get lucky with something and make a giant progressive leap forward. However, more often luck is just a happy coincidence of being in the right place at the right time.

When we take a giant leap with luck, most times we don't know how we did it and without striking luck again, we can't reproduce the process. Since we don't really understand what we did to land in our new spot, we often end up stumbling backwards in our journey.

The wisdom that is gained from being present during every small step of your journey is what will carry you through your life. There is no price that can be placed on the value of learning and the insight it brings to your life. When you know more, you can do more. As you learn to own your awesome, it becomes easier to increase your knowledge and bring wisdom into a variety of circumstances.

Think of owning your awesome as a manufacturing process and the learning that happens at each step as the assembly line. The process of production is the knowledge that you build through each life experience. However, the wisdom gained is uncovering how those experiences have impacted your overall life. The assembly line is the constant journey to own your awesome.

> The wisdom that is gained from being present during every small step of your journey is what will carry you through your life.

THE EASY BUTTON

I am like everyone else, I love to find the easy button! I love to find the fastest way from point A to point C and if I can figure out a way to skip B, I will. I am always on the lookout for a better way.

There is nothing wrong with that and in many cases, I am a big believer in process improvement for business, efficiency, and family life to name a few. Unfortunately, the journey to owning your awesome has no real shortcuts or easy buttons as it requires you to live as many experiences as possible and learn about yourself in a deeper way.

Your attitude and aptitude can play a major role in making it a smoother process from beginning to celebration time. Owning your awesome is a mindset that takes work, patience and resiliency. With bold courage, you will and must learn things about yourself and others along the way as that plays a big part in how you will evolve and grow. You must understand that you can't bring about wisdom overnight.

Your learning often has to be broken down into smaller experiences that are built upon because if it is absorbed with too big of a learning curve, you may choke, literally and figuratively. Learning about yourself is valuable so you can work through those things that threaten to hold you back. It takes time and the willingness to proceed to be grateful for every bit of progress you achieve.

For me, the inability to hit the easy button is one of the hardest pills for me to swallow in this prescription for owning your awesome. Because of my keen brain for ideation I often thought I could see ways around the learning process. That meant avoiding what I call those prickly moments or points that hold you back from your destination. I tried to race around (and skip the wisdom-building part) to get to the next point.

However, because I hadn't learned what I needed to learn in an earlier experience, I would find myself right back where I started. Life has a way of making sure you learn important lessons and the more you fight it, the more recurrences seem to occur.

I love entertaining and I love to cook. Cooking for me is a time for relaxation, creativity and me time. I love experimenting with spices and new dishes or ways to present the dish in an appealing manner to my family and guests. I am often able to cook without the need for recipes and can reproduce delicious and appetizing meals thanks to my mother who has always been a passionate foodie.

> Life has a way of making sure you learn important lessons and the more you fight it, the more recurrences seem to occur.

Baking is another story entirely. I have attempted many times to just wing it when I bake and the outcome has been certainly less than perfect. As an adoring mother, I have regretted trying to improvise on recipes as I was making a birthday cake for my children over the years.

The thing with baking is that if you do follow the directions and go through the process, it will most often turn out perfect every time. The recipe is tried and true and has been proven to work. If that's the case, then why do I always try to buck the system and attempt to customize it or fast track it, knowing the chances of failing are high?

I started thinking about how proud I am when one of my baking projects turns out well. There is nothing like presenting your guests with a stunning desert, the piece de resistance of the meal. I liken my baking experience to my journey to owning my awesome. I can skip the steps if I want to. However, it may force me to start over from scratch and do it again. What if I created a recipe for owning my awesome so that I could be more confident about how I lead each day, knowing that implementing this recipe with bold courage would result in a fresh baked life of happiness, satisfaction and a level of fulfillment I had never known before? Would it be worth the effort to try? It is for me.

I am once again reminded of the little boy saving the starfish as I recognized that if there was ever a moment to develop a new discipline for saving me from undue stress and failure, this was the time for bold courage and writing my recipe for success. If the child's efforts saved a starfish one at a time, then in reality, my efforts combined with the right plan should save me and lead me to a more joyful, fulfilled and satisfied life. That would put me in a state of being able to consistently do the right thing time and time again.

PART 3

A CASE CALLED WORTHY

CHAPTER 14

SECRET TO BEING A GAME CHANGER

Nothing great ever comes from allowing or accepting mediocrity. When you aim for mediocre, you only ever achieve mediocre and that is if you're lucky. If you miss your aim of mediocre even slightly you get even less.

The acceptance of mediocrity is a very expensive decision in your life and the cost of that decision is disappointment.

Many of the things in my life that still haunt me are those times when I was disappointed or when I regretted not striving for my best and accepting less than my most valiant effort. Regret is a powerful emotion that can be debilitating when it comes to the pursuit of our dreams. The best way to avoid that is to go after and own our awesome.

One emotion more powerful than regret is satisfaction. Being satisfied that you are doing everything in your power to live boldly and strive towards your awesome will help ward off any regrets. I challenge you, right now, to aim for that juicy, succulent life that you think may be out of your reach. I'm here to tell you – anything is possible. Just ask Barrack

> The acceptance of mediocrity is a very expensive decision in your life and the cost of that decision is disappointment.

Obama, the first African American President of the United States. His path of incredibly hard work and focus had to be endured to get him to the highest office in the American nation.

Annie Oakley, Martin Luther King, Joan of Arc, Steve Jobs, and Nelson Mandela all had something in common. They were all game changers in their own right. There are many other names I could list as famous game changers. They aren't hard to spot because they always stand out from the crowd.

They are those individuals who challenged mediocrity and went for excellence, bucking the system in some way to change the trajectory of society. They went after their own satisfaction regardless of what society said they should be able to do.

Each of them was a pioneer under difficult and sometimes seemingly impossible circumstances. They rose to the occasion and pushed through barriers and limiting beliefs and made a big impact not only in their own lives, but also in those around them.

Whether their occasion was to break through gender, race or societal biases isn't relevant for our purposes. The important thing to grasp is that they all had obstacles to overcome, up to and including battling an entire nation's thinking.

For example, Mandela was convicted of conspiracy to overthrow a corrupt government and then imprisoned for 27 years, yet he held fast to his belief in a better government for Africa and eventually orchestrated that dream to come to fruition. Oakley was the first performing woman sharp shooter in an era when all her female colleagues were solely home makers. Steve Jobs broke all technology barriers at the helm of the Apple Empire.

These innovators thought differently and saw possibility for their increased satisfaction and gave themselves permission to go after their goals.

The interesting thing about satisfaction is that the more you achieve, the more you want, and the more you are willing to do to go after it.

In our research studies on employee engagement and how it relates to satisfaction, it was clearly proven that when people are more satisfied, they are more productive. Conversely, when people are more productive, they are more satisfied, thus creating a continual positive effect feedback loop.

Just because you don't have to face corruption, the fear of going to prison, or try to overcome racial biases doesn't mean you don't have a mission in front of you. I am challenging you right now to become a game changer in your own life.

Right now, if you want to own your awesome you need to rise to the occasion of your own life and claim it. Accept the beauty that comes when you challenge yourself to resist mediocrity and aim for greatness. Aim for full satisfaction with every moment; don't settle for any mediocrity in your life.

Your life is like a great meal. Imagine if you sat down to eat and discovered that the chef avoided stirring any spices in the preparation of the food. Instead, he or she kept them all together in one little corner of the dish.

You would end up having some very spicy bits, some bland tasteless bits, and other bits that were just perfect. The problem would be that you wouldn't know which bites were going to be great and which ones wouldn't be worth absorbing the calories to consume.

You could end up eating until you were full without finding more than one perfectly satisfying bite. What a disappointment!

Don't allow your life to be full of too spicy or too bland bites. Instead, go for a perfectly seasoned, juicy bite and then another and another!

Enjoy every moment knowing with full satisfaction that every bite can be just as good as the one before it.

When I decided I wanted to make all areas of my life more satisfying, it changed my world. Just like a well prepared meal, now I never settle and I always demand the best bites!

I am always inspired hearing stories of young children stating with absolute confidence and clarity that they want to be President, a rocket scientist or a famous actor. They say it with such conviction, heart and passion that it is believable. Somewhere along the journey of maturing our hopes and dreams and what we believe possible, we can lose our passion. Now is the time to claim it back and fan its flames.

Give yourself permission to say "yes!" Allow yourself to get excited and ignited about your future. Don't hold back in any area. Go for everything you have dreamed of with a belief that it is possible. Striving for excellence requires bold courage.

I am not advocating that you strive for perfection, which is demotivating and usually unattainable. When you decide to own your awesome, inadvertently you decide to aim for excellence. Excellence in all areas of developing your awesome gets better with age and practice. The more you work at something, the better you get. The better your personal best gets, the more elevated your definition of excellence gets. See the pattern developing here?

Patterns are powerful and our brains are complex, but once our brain understands and selects a pattern, it holds it tight. There are some scientific reasons and explanations about the topic of your brain and neuropathways, but the most important part to know right now is that when something becomes a habit, our brains develop pathways that make it easier to accept that habit and make it harder to break it. But it is not impossible.

No matter our age, gender, socioeconomic status or race, people are creatures of habit. These habits become our own rules of conduct. By our nature we like to stay within our comfort zones and we follow self-imposed rules both consciously and unconsciously. This is evident even when it comes to simple things, like choosing a seat in church or ordering a certain lunch from an often visited restaurant. We find ourselves returning to the same seat and ordering our favorite foods.

Because of these habits, we spend part of our lives just going through motions, not living in full satisfaction or questioning our choices. We exist within the status quo and life seems good enough.

I am challenging you to ask yourself more questions, like, "would it make me happier to sit nearer to the front in church to have a more up-close experience?"

This may seem like a trivial change, but it is necessary to start with small questions about our habits and how they make us happy before we move into more dramatic areas of life in our search for satisfaction. That is because satisfaction itself is habit forming.

If you can increase your satisfaction levels in your life, you won't want to accept anything less going forward.

I was having a conversation with a friend the other day. She was going through a tough time and had been hit with a series of misfortunes through no fault of her own. She told me how she wanted to have more joy, satisfaction and fun in her life. She then said that she thinks she has forgotten what that looks like for her.

That got me to thinking about our satisfaction in life and what we put up with. Many of us are just going through the motions of living. There is nothing satisfying or awesome about moving through the motions of life. There is comfort there, but not for the long term. Over the years, such an approach to living just leads to disappointment for all the things you didn't do or try.

TWO SETS OF RULES?

Years ago on my quest to own my awesome I realized that I had one set of standards that was set for myself and one that I held for the rest of the world. When I compared the two sets of rules, the ones I had for myself were much more stringent and the consequences of breaking one were larger than the expectations I had for others.

The standards that I held myself to were very high. I am not talking about the kind of high standards that I encouraged you to recognize is possible for you in an effort to cast out mediocrity. I am talking about the kind of high standards that caused restraint in my actions, tore down my confidence and disallowed joy. These were the kind of standards where I made judgments about myself with a much stricter measuring stick than the one I used to measure others.

In the midst of being strict with myself, I suddenly realized one day that I was watching others live their dreams, I was sitting back with restraint for the fear of looking silly or having others judge me as harshly as I judged myself. I was striving for my own excellence, but my self-definition of excellence was hundreds of feet higher than everyone else's.

Consider when you look at photos of yourself, you are inclined to point out your flaws. You think you are too fat, too pale, too dark under the eyes, too old or whatever other criticism you can muster up about yourself. Yet you often measure the other people in the photo much less harshly, and find their beauty and joy in that moment. Being able to see yourself in that light is a sure way to measure if you are on your way to owning your awesome. Remember you aren't striving for perfection; rather you are consistently striving for excellence.

We are too hard on ourselves and most times don't allow ourselves the freedom to live fully. We look at others and admire their spirit to get out there and try things and risk looking silly. We encourage them to dust themselves off and try again if they make an error. We need to do the same for ourselves. The punishment for making a mistake or for looking silly isn't death nor should it be unending self-loathing and remorse.

You already know that in order to fully embrace and accept this journey to owning your awesome you are going to have to stretch out of that negative zone and live fully. Break some rules, blaze a trail

Chapter 14

over new ground, ignite your spirit and give yourself permission to be actively engaged in your life. Have the courage to say yes to yourself, and allow yourself the same grace that you lovingly give others. The secret to being a game changer starts and ends with you.

> The secret to being a game changer starts and ends with you.

PART 4

THE QUEST FOR SUCCESS

CHAPTER 15

YOUR STORY MEANS SOMETHING

Some of the best speakers and leaders that I respect in society today are those who share their stories.

Everyone has a number of stories forming an integral web that has been woven from the threads of their life history. Our experiences and the resulting story have relevance and meaning to more than just us. When we look at stories of others we gain insight into what they believe in and who they are as people.

Similarly, our stories help people get a better understanding and appreciation for who we are and what makes us tick. Most importantly, when we look at our own stories we can appreciate and understand ourselves better and give ourselves grace as well.

Your human experiences and your level of satisfaction in evaluating your experiences are an integral part of the journey to owning your awesome. The way we perceive our life moments can be crucial to our level of success or failure in future years.

Years ago my husband and I took a trip for the purpose of having a quiet retreat with each other to plan and envision our year ahead. Prior to the trip I planned some exercises for us to be creative and to create discussion about what our future would look like.

I created an exercise that I called the Time Capsule Blueprint. I didn't know it at the time, but that exercise was a game changer for how I was going to make decisions and it deeply impacted my world going forward. It has ended up being a tool that I continue to build upon to achieve incredible results and own my awesome.

The exercise of the Time Capsule Blueprint was one that we each took on individually to capture our memories and timelines of our own lives. It started with the intention of a one-day exercise, but it turned into a week-long focus. The exercise helped encapsulate the memories of each of our lives in our own documents, but it also created an incredible feeling of satisfaction for me to realize the things I had accomplished throughout my life.

It was all there in black and white, the good, the bad, the ugly as well as the beautiful moments of my life. As I read my document, I was able to share and celebrate the wins in my life and also give thanks for the lessons I learned through those times where I was challenged or I stumbled.

As humans we often see and recall our failures first and with the Time Capsule Blueprint exercise I was able to overcome my feelings of failure and accept them as part of the bigger picture of my life.

Before my eyes something transformed, and that was the value of my life story. By creating that simple document, my perceived failures were overshadowed by the number of stories that are worth telling and that are each a part of what makes me who I am today. The process also gave me a deeper understanding of patterns that could be seen in my life that I could choose to avoid in the new version of owning my awesome.

There are some things best left in the past and some things I should carry with me to my future. Through the blueprint I realized there were times that I carried many of the negative things with me and not enough of the positive. Now I had the ability to change that thinking.

It's a simple process to complete the Time Capsule Blueprint, but I will warn you it is a bit time consuming in the beginning and it is addictive. As you work up to current day events it becomes simple and very quick to keep it updated. To get started, all you have to do is make a simple chart with two columns. The title of the first column should be "age range." In that column write out your age in 5 year increments starting with 0-5 years, then 6-10, 11-15 and so on, until you reach your current age.

This will make it easier for you, because our minds aren't finite and date stamped with our memories and we aren't always able to zero in on the exact date. Date ranges are much easier to recall, and it doesn't affect the process or your results at all.

In the second column of the document put the title "my experiences." In this second column write down all of your life highlights and lowlights that you can remember. There will be more entries and it will be easier to remember events as you get closer to your actual age. That is normal, as all of our memory banks get a little fuzzy with time. As you get started don't worry about the chronological order of events. Simply put them down as they come to your mind in the appropriate boxes where they fit.

Through the Time Capsule Blueprint you are able to assess your own experiences and actions for the purpose of learning and development. This process is extremely valuable for increasing personal fulfillment and satisfaction because you will see and understand yourself more objectively. By reviewing all of your life experiences and capturing them resume style, you will find pride and satisfaction in taking stock of your journey thus far.

You will be reminded of the beauty in your life, acknowledge the experiences that were painful and forgive and praise yourselves as you go. You will be able to see that every experience in your life was a unique story that collectively meshes together to form the mosaic of your life. It is like a thumbprint showcasing your one of a kind life.

Stories create trust and a connection with an audience, a team, a partner or anyone else. Stories build trust that goes far deeper than just training or selling; they create camaraderie and connection. Personal stories connect to emotions and emotions are what showcase our personalities, our values, our biases and the lens in which we see our world.

As a professional speaker I already knew the impact that a powerful story could make, so it wasn't a complete surprise, but the Time Capsule Blueprint helped me realize the need to share more of my own life stories. They are both a testament to my life and to my ability to have an impact to help others. I was overjoyed at that thought of impacting others, as part of owning my awesome meant having a larger impact on those around me.

When I was finished reflecting on my completed Time Capsule Blueprint, I had developed and anchored a much deeper sense of who I was. It was easy to see what I brought to any situation going forward, from my experiences, my skills and my heart. I had context of my whole life and not just a few quick broken-up stories.

It was an interesting exercise but it also became more than that for me. This process kick-started a time of healing and of confidence building. I also felt a dramatic increase in my well- being, knowing that I truly had something to offer the world. Everything that I had experienced so far had value and brought me wisdom that I otherwise may not have had. I found extreme pride in who I was and still am and the proof of the effort I have made in my lifetime so far.

Since that first attempt at the blueprint I have continued filling it in to this day. My values in how I live my life have been reaffirmed and that has brought a new appreciation for every step of my journey. Essentially now that my story has been captured in my bullet point version of my autobiography also known as my Time Capsule Blueprint, I use this bullet point list as a reminder for me when I am speaking to an audience.

I build out stories where I think I can help people that day depending on the topic.

Humans have an incredible capacity to bounce back from loss and to experience the joys of life. We have the capacity to be resilient warriors and can be courageous when we have to be. The Time Capsule Blueprint is not only a useful tool, but the process of doing the exercise gave me a true appreciation and satisfaction in my life's work so far. It allowed me an opportunity to frame everything and I see me in a new perspective of where I came from. I also dream of where I could go in my future. Would we put a picture of the Blueprint if we are making an associated workbook or just allow the diagram of the Blueprint to be in the workbook?

POWER IN YOUR STORY

There is a blog that I really love to read called Humans of New York. The Founder, Brandon Stanton, launched it in 2010 with the intention of photographing and writing about 10,000 random inhabitants of New York. He thought it would be cool to give the world a glimpse into the melting pot of what New York living offers. He took a picture and quoted his subjects sharing something with him about their life and the wisdom they gained from it.

An amazing thing started to happen. People were interested in other people's stories and wanted to celebrate the human spirit. Strangers started engaging and sharing the posts as somehow they appreciated and connected with the authentic story of the randomly highlighted people.

With more than twenty million social media followers, Humans of New York offers a glimpse into people's lives and a short story about each of them. The power of the human story gives voice to people's lives and creates connection when people need hope and peace, knowing there are others who have walked similar journeys as well.

A crucial step to owning your awesome is going through this process of reflection and owning and finding value and power in your own story. Through reflection and understanding, you can validate yourself, your experiences and restore your own confidence. Consider the Time Capsule Blueprint a framework for a series of events that have power to elicit various emotions that are unique to your life and the character of who you are, how you have changed or stayed the same and who you desire to become.

CHALLENGE ON!

I challenge you to do the process of taking the time to capture your own Time Capsule Blueprint. When you take stock of your life's milestones and become more aware of them, you will automatically start to increase your appreciation for your life.

There is freedom that comes with owning your truth, the stories of who you are and what you have experienced. There is freedom is letting down your walls of pretending to be something more or less than what you are.

Learn to stand in your truth, embrace your authentic stories and start living more intentionally. By continuing your story it sets the stage for living your blueprint in real time and that is where life gets exciting. Bold courage can take flight, and you will be cognizant of the experiences you choose and what will be worthwhile and make you proud to add to your blueprint. Have bold courage to stretch your limits, to embrace and conquer those temporary fears and to acknowledge your daily wins and losses, as they are part of your living history.

PART 4

THE QUEST FOR SUCCESS

CHAPTER 16

PERFECTLY FLAWED

Life is like an egg. Eggs are sometimes raw, other times hard boiled, scrambled, or sunny side up. Life is too! Just like people prefer different states of eggs, they also prefer different stages of life over others. Sometimes your life is raw, hard, scrambled up and devoid of sense and other days it is sunny side up and all is well.

Finding the perfect egg is nearly as impossible as finding the perfect life. It's never easy to accept that our lives are fallible and flawed, but the reality is, they are. I've never met a person yet who has come through life unscathed by their experiences. Everyone has skeletons in their closet that they would rather forget or things they wish had turned out differently.

Some of you will have experiences included in your Time Capsule Blueprint that cause you to feel shame or remorse. You may wish you could erase them or never have to talk about them again.

All humans are inclined to use silence as the ultimate weapon of power. We keep silent and don't allow anyone to see our errors or our potential perceived flaws. We fear rejection or judgment by our loved ones, by our colleagues and even by perfect strangers. Because of fear we hide behind our perfectly crafted persona keeping silent and burying those pieces of ourselves we don't feel proud of.

We keep things hidden and bottled up inside for fear that someone might find out about our flaws. We build walls to keep people out so they don't discover the true us.

The trouble with this is that when you build walls to keep people out, in effect you build a box around yourself and it traps you in. You close yourself into a place of being less than your awesome and not owning your identity to live your life fully. Most times, keeping things locked up inside causes us more harm than good and we live a lifetime carrying shame and enduring low self-esteem.

Who needs that or wants that? What I have learned through my journey with bold courage is that real power comes in being open about my flaws. When I face the fear that others won't love me or even like me because of something they see in my cracked shell, I gain strength in who I am. Just like the egg whose shell is marred, it didn't change the taste of the egg or what the egg can be used for. I have learned that giving all of my flaws and experiences a voice if needed to share wisdom has been freeing for me. I have never believed that I should hide the parts of myself that are less than perfect. Those people I choose to allow around me must accept me for who I am, flaws, quirks and all. My relationships are so much deeper and more authentic that way.

You needn't be like me and share everything and give voice to your flaws publicly. Nonetheless, you will have to come to terms with yourself with all of your flaws and brokenness on some levels. You do need to recognize and accept that although you might not be perfect, you are worthy of all the great things you desire.

I'm suggesting replacing silence as the ultimate weapon of power with acceptance. There is far more power in allowing yourself to feel the satisfaction and acceptance of the life you have lived so far, than in hiding it. Life may not have gone as planned, but you came through it.

Your relationship with yourself determines your relationship with everything and everyone else. If you don't love and accept yourself, it is very difficult for anyone else to do it. Your self-loathing puts a strain on all your relationships.

I am confident in saying that most everyone's version of owning their awesome includes other people in their life. Having people who you can trust and spend time with sharing experiences and love are precious. Even the most independent people want and need love. It is difficult to have healthy trusting relationships with others without accepting yourself fully first and allowing them to do the same.

Often, we hold back pieces of ourselves either consciously or unconsciously and by doing that we aren't allowing our loved ones to accept us for who we are. To ensure you have healthy relationships with those around you, ensure you have a healthy relationship with yourself first. Be honest with yourself and about the things that upset you or cause you to feel some shame. At the same time, allow yourself to celebrate the things throughout your life that have brought you immense joy and satisfaction.

At times you may also be tempted to hide those joyful moments and keep them safely tucked away from others so as to avoid any judgments or tarnishes on what you hold precious. You give away your own power by fearing judgments.

When you can't accept who you are and all of the experiences that come with your life, the good, the bad and the in-between, it affects your self-esteem. You start to build walls around certain areas of your life and isolate those areas that are vulnerable. The walls are thick and seem to get thicker over time, making it increasingly difficult for anyone to penetrate.

With bold courage you can break down any walls you have created around yourself by accepting who you have been in the past, who you are now and who you look forward to becoming in the future. Accept yourself and your story as being your whole truth and embrace the understanding that it is a beautiful part of who you are. When you do this your level of satisfaction will rise.

Throughout my career thus far, I have seen all spectrums of effort from those simply living their journey all the way up to stepping into and owning their awesome. I have come to the conclusion that acceptance is the key to lasting success when it comes to celebrating our gifts and our flaws. After countless conversations and strategies built to help people own their awesome it was easy to see that no amount of self-help can ever make up for anybody's shortage of self-acceptance. The more you can accept yourself and look at your life with a more meaningful purpose, the easier it is to own your awesome. You recognize that your life may not have gone as planned, but you have prevailed over every area of your life so far. All the pieces of your stories are what make you unique, strong, resilient individuals and because of this you carry far more self-esteem.

> After countless conversations and strategies built to help people own their awesome it was easy to see that no amount of self-help can ever make up for anybody's shortage of self-acceptance.

SELF-ESTEEM VERSUS SELF-CONFIDENCE

When I refer to self-esteem it should not be mistaken as being the same thing as self-confidence. There is a big difference between the two.

Self-esteem refers to how you feel about yourself in the overall big picture of life. It refers to how much esteem, or positive reflection or self-worth, that you have. Self-esteem develops from nurtured experiences and situations that have shaped how you view yourself today. It is a measure of what you think you are worth.

A quick way to do a check in about your level of self-esteem is to reflect on things you say or think about yourself when prompted. If you find yourself being overly critical of yourself, putting yourself down, using negative talk in reference to yourself or maybe allowing other people to dictate your worth by accepting what they say about you, that is a good indicator that your self-esteem is low. If your self-esteem is low your satisfaction is most likely low too and you need to make some changes.

You can have low self-esteem, yet at the same time have high self-confidence. Self-esteem is not an indicator of the level of self-confidence someone feels. However, increasing your self-confidence can increase your self-esteem.

This might seem a little confusing, but I assure you it is simpler than it sounds. Self-confidence is your sense of ability to do a task or perform an act; it is about action. Think of self-confidence as it grows after the number of times you have done a task. The task could be anything and range in complexity from knitting to brain surgery. The number of times you have done this task successfully in the past will dictate your level of self confidence in successfully doing it again.

For example, someone can be an excellent golfer who can come in under par every game and their self confidence is high about their ability to succeed at golf. But they still have low self-esteem because they don't feel like a worthwhile human being in the world.

The good news is you can increase both confidence and esteem in yourself and it is easy to get started. To increase self-esteem, the first step is to stop the negative chatter about yourself. That's the internal dialogue you have going on in your head about yourself and also those you give voice to externally. Fully accept who you are and every piece of your story as a valuable bit of wisdom you've gathered to lead you somewhere better. That will make a world of difference in your self-esteem if you do just that one thing.

To increase your self-confidence you will need to increase your skills for the task, but first make a list of all the things you are naturally trained to be good at. Look at areas where you find success and feel fulfilled when you are done.

Next make a list of things you want to be good at and have more confidence in that will help you own your awesome.

Once you have your two lists, celebrate the list of things that you feel confident in and take stock of the list detailing those things in which you wish to gain confidence. Figure out ways that you can increase your skills and confidence. It could be as simple as getting a little more practice or maybe you need to seek some outside help and get some lessons or training. Start with each item one at a time and see how your confidence grows in proportion to your skillset.

Both self-esteem and self-confidence have the ability to increase your satisfaction, but self-confidence can only take it so far. Your true satisfaction is limited by your level of self-esteem.

So as you finish your Time Capsule Blueprint take some time to pat yourself on the back and fully accept all that has happened to date. Embrace each moment throughout your life as though it was preparing you to go somewhere great. It was! It was preparing you to own your awesome.

THE STORY OF AMANDA

This past weekend, I attended a women's conference and was really struck by the wisdom and the ability of the speaker to tell her story. She was raw, authentic and dramatic throughout her presentation. She shared the story of her life growing up that was nothing like the sweet fairy tales we read to our children.

She lived through some rough times, some that were thrust upon her and others she admittedly created. She told of how she made choices that were not in her best interest at the time and landed herself in some places she didn't want to be. Her level of satisfaction even as a young girl was very low and her self-esteem had been severely damaged by her dysfunctional family life. She held herself in low regard for years and didn't feel like she had much to offer the world.

To her credit, in her 30s she recognized the pattern happening in her life and decided to change the trajectory and own her life. She wanted more. She shared her feelings about this coming of wisdom and her decision to own her awesome and find her voice. She stood confidently before hundreds of people and rather than skim over the parts of the story that were unflattering to her, she marched right through them verbally with a contagious self-acceptance.

Everyone applauded her transparency and nobody judged her for any mistake she said she made in her journey. Quite the opposite happened. The audience was refreshed by her willingness to share her vulnerability and it made it easy to join her in acceptance of everything. She received huge applause and I know for a fact she touched many audience members that day who may have been feeling ashamed or had tucked away certain parts of themselves for safe keeping. Through her willingness to share her flaws, she made it easier for others to do the same and gain a renewal of self-esteem in the process.

PART 4

THE QUEST FOR SUCCESS

CHAPTER 17

THE ART OF GIVING

I love serving others and giving back is an integral part of how I own my awesome. Many times throughout my adult life I have taken on projects to raise awareness and/or funds for several different charities. I have learned that what fills my soul is when I am able to help others as it leaves me feeling more fulfilled and connected to the heart of who I am. When I help others it is like something magical happens and my heart expands and everything seems a little bit more right with the world that day.

The projects that I have chosen to take part in to give back over the years have brought me tremendous pride knowing that in some way I could make a difference. Philanthropy has always been a major goal of mine and I invest in charitable organizations monetarily as well as through my efforts as often as I can.

I enter each project asking myself two questions. The first is: "What is the desired impact of the project?" The second is: "What ways could I participate or give of my efforts to make it happen?"

I ask these questions to ensure that the project is in alignment with my skills and abilities, as well as my heart. While it is true that other people's lives or organizations are changed when I give, the bigger picture and further understanding is that when I give, I am changed as well. Through my desire to help others, I've actually received gifts that money can't buy. These are presents to the heart and soul. In my desire to be of service to others, I was changed in countless ways and for that I will be forever grateful.

You are likely thinking you are too busy to give time to an individual in need or a charitable organization, or maybe you feel too strapped for cash to donate money. But I assure you there are many ways to give with varying levels of time, effort and responsibility. At different moments during my life, I have had varying amounts of time and finances to be able to give to others. However, even with a busy career and often hectic travel schedule, I have always been able to find ways to lend a hand on some level.

Obviously I was able to give more when I had more, and my level of happiness and fulfillment did rise with the more I was able to do. When I miss the opportunity to give back I feel as though there is a piece of the puzzle missing. The feeling that something isn't quite right will plague me leaving me wondering what I have forgotten, until I realize that I need to look outside myself and remedy the situation. The role I play in an effort for an organization has varied, as well, over the years. When I have more time, I give more time and when I have more money, I give more money. I give as much as I can and as often as I can.

GIVING BIGGER

Something that has brought me a great deal of satisfaction is when my team and I decided that our idea of giving back needed to go to the next level. Many years ago we started a foundation that provides for those less fortunate. Some of the ways we contribute are with our time, our professional skills and with monetary support to many organizations and individuals that need assistance.

One of our upcoming endeavors is organizing a mission trip to take a team of skilled leaders to a developing country to assist in developing sustainable permaculture. We will work together over the course of a couple of weeks and bring some much needed development of agriculture ecosystems to some of the more needy villages.

While we are there we will bring hope, financial means, labor, education, and support and we will implement strategies for more sustainable living. Our efforts in tandem with the locals will increase quality of life to approximately 200 families living in a very remote setting.

Studies have proven that when we give to others something mystical happens in our brains that isn't triggered or reproduced by doing any other act. Our brains release endorphins into our systems that send out positive energy that make you feel particularly good after completing a meaningful deed.

It is similar to the effect of a good physical workout in that both acts make you feel physically and emotionally fulfilled. In the case of giving this is commonly referred to as "helper high." It is a distinct sensation where when people give they feel stronger, more energetic, calmer and have stronger feelings of self-worth.

Additionally, a 2016 study published in Psychosomatic Medicine Journal of Biobehavioral *Medicine* found that giving has a positive effect on key brain areas involved in stress and reward responses.

All of those feelings are side effects that will support your journey to owning your awesome.

Deeper feelings of satisfaction are also side effects of being altruistic and helping others. Many will debate that if you really look at the benefits of giving, which are equally as high to the person giving as the person receiving, perhaps it isn't purely altruistic.

I see the act of giving as a beautiful cycle where we can all win.

Just because you are giving doesn't mean you shouldn't feel good about it. You most certainly should feel great that you are making a difference for another. Embrace that feeling knowing that you deserve it. The notion that everybody benefits from helping each other is one that I certainly embrace and will continue to allow myself to feel the joy and pride when doing great things for others. It's an added perk if I can feel better about myself at the same time.

Another way that helping others will increase your satisfaction is that when we start to think of others and turn our eyes off ourselves, we become more grateful for what we have. The old saying about the grass being greener on the other side seems true until you stand on the other grass. Once you experience what others are going through, even though it may have appeared greener on their side, you realize that everyone has their issues and interestingly enough, when they looked at your grass they may have thought yours looked greener.

Gratitude for our own lives is enhanced by challenging our assumptions about others and really seeing what they are going through and facing in their lives. When you focus on others it also becomes a good distraction and keeps your mind busy instead of concentrating on your own problems.

THE ART OF RECEIVING

From a young age, it is ingrained in us to think it is better to give than to receive. Consequently many of us are expert givers and lousy receivers. In a world that rewards giving we simply have never learned how to receive. The notion that the act of giving is better than the act of receiving is confusing to me because for every person who gives there needs to be at least one person to receive. You can't have one without the other. When we don't allow ourselves to receive we also deny the person who is trying to give the pleasure of fully giving.

When we are not open to receiving we aren't open to fully enjoy the depths of our relationships. To limit others in giving to you robs them and you of a very important part of your relationship with each other and throws off the balance between you and giving and taking.

There are a few reasons why you may have difficulty receiving, the first being you may not be very practiced at it. You also may not want to be seen as a taker and the third is that by receiving, you make yourself vulnerable by allowing someone else to help you.

Of course all of these reasons have no basis in fact; they are just your own ego getting in the way.

When you let your pride and judgments go, it will allow you to accept and even enjoy being on the receiving side of things once in a while.

I remember a time during the Christmas season not that long ago when I met a family who had a roof over their head, but not much else. It was a serendipitous meeting, as I had been looking for a second-hand large stand-up popcorn maker. I answered an online ad that the mother of the family posted. She wrote me back and assured me that the machine was clean and in excellent condition so I agreed to go and buy it from her the next morning.

When I arrived at her home, I was taken back by the conditions of the house. It was very run down with no wall coverings or light fixtures and just bare wood for floors. She led me to the kitchen area and on the way I passed several dark rooms filled with children who were wrapped up in blankets. I still wasn't clueing in as to the depth of need for this family until I got to the kitchen and noticed that all four burners of her stove were turned on high and burning hot, but there were no pots on the stove and she wasn't cooking anything.

I remember saying to her that they were on and was there something wrong with her stove/ I thought it must have shorted and turned itself on, to which she replied that she had no heat in the house because she couldn't afford to pay the gas bill so she was trying to get some heat from the stove burners.

This was in Canada and it is extremely cold here in the winter. People freeze to death if they aren't properly protected against the bitter cold. Imagine my shock and feeling of embarrassment as I shrunk into my jacket a little further as she shared with me her plight of no heat.

I felt so bad for pointing out what should have been obvious to me, that the house had no heat and was freezing. She brought out the popcorn maker and as I looked at it I tried not to gasp because it truly was a mess. The inside was dirty and it had broken knobs and was in overall poor repair. It was nothing like she had described it to be to me, nor was it really what I was hoping for. But as I stood in her kitchen that day I explained that it was perfect and I would take it.

My caveat to purchasing it was that I wanted to pay her twice what she was asking because it was such a "fine" machine. The look on the mother's face said it all; she gratefully accepted my money and helped me take the machine to the car. I saw the hope and joy that came across her face that day by a simple gesture on my part, and suddenly I was the giver and she the receiver.

She appreciated the extra money and I know it meant a great deal to help support her family. I felt satisfied leaving there and having been able to assist a family in need. I took that popcorn maker home and spent hours scrubbing it up and bringing it back to life. I left the broken knobs as a reminder of that day. Every time I look at that popcorn maker I am reminded that there is a grace in being able to receive, just as that mother had.

Later that holiday season, I was able to take some of our Foundation's holiday drive money and outfit that same family with hundreds of dollars in cash and plenty of supplies and food for the holidays. We had gone shopping and filled several large grocery carts with every kind of food you can imagine. My team and I delivered that food about a week before Christmas and it was glorious.

The mother was shocked and in awe, yet she so graciously accepted the unexpected gift on behalf of her family and that made it easy for us to give to her. We left feeling like champions who were able to help out and she felt excitement about being able to feed her kids and enjoy some healthy food over the holidays. It was so interesting to me that in her willingness to receive she actually gave us a gift – the gift of being able to give. We felt pure joy!

Let the notion that she give us the gift of being able to give to her sink in for a moment. Had she protested and said we didn't need to do that or been awkward about things (when in reality she needed the money and the food), it wouldn't have been as exciting or as successful for our team.

Our team left her place feeling a little bit better about themselves and walking a little taller that day. That's what it is all about for me. Finding and owning my awesome and helping others to do the same is a place I love to be. Sometimes instead of giving you have to receive so everyone can find their awesome and feel the satisfaction of being fulfilled.

PART 5

LEADING THE SHIFT

CHAPTER 18

EMPOWERMENT THROUGH FEEDBACK

Feedback has no value unless it leads to improvement. The road to owning your awesome is always paved with improvement, so feedback is a critical part of your journey. Remember, owning your awesome is not necessarily an end destination. It is more of a lifestyle of improvement. Lifestyles are like plants in that they need to be assessed, cultivated and pruned regularly to ensure that they stay on track with growth and fortitude. Your awesome lifestyle needs to be maintained and assessed and feedback must be gathered regularly.

When you have an opportunity to gain feedback from a credible source, seize that moment! In that moment there is an opportunity for reflection, growth and improvement for your journey. Feedback is important in many aspects if used correctly. By accepting feedback, you are able to identify the strengths and weaknesses of any situation, journey or even personal aspects of yourself. Feedback is extremely important to consider on your journey to owning your awesome.

As you gather external feedback (which is feedback received from others), you can compare it to your own assessment (internal feedback)

> Feedback has no value unless it leads to improvement.

of any situation. When you review both types of feedback and the information revealed it is an opportunity to see if the feedback is aligned or disconnected.

If it isn't aligned you should review the reason why that might be. Perhaps the person you received the external feedback from has an unclear view of the situation or perhaps your own lens is clouded. By reviewing the feedback there is an opportunity for you to grow as a person on the path you have taken. Or you may decide it is time to take another look and make some changes. Either way, progress and improvement are made.

My favorite two aspects of feedback include the ability to learn what went right and what went wrong in any situation and how I am performing.

In both aspects there is room for personal future growth and change if I allow it. To welcome improvement, I have to remain open to what the feedback has to tell me. If I am open, I can use the feedback to figure out what went wrong if it isn't going as planned or alternatively decipher the brilliance of what is going right and do more of that. By considering these notions, I have an opportunity to improve my level of owning my awesome as I journey forward and I can also avoid any possible sticky situations by using my knowledge of the past. Either way I accept, reflect and try and learn from all feedback. The same holds true for you.

TIME CAPSULE BLUEPRINT FEEDBACK

The document that you have created with all of your life memories written down is now a very useful source for personal feedback. As you review your historical timeline of the happenings in your life, I encourage you to remember a few things. Understand that no matter what it says in your time capsule, you are not just the sum of your worst mistakes; you are so much more than that.

Read your story as a whole and not just in single pieces. You have nothing to prove to anyone and the darker parts of your journey hold great value, perhaps even rivaling the value of the bright shining moments for learning. You should also recognize that you have value in the grand scheme of things.

Not everything that happened in your life was about you. In fact, at times you were just a player in the larger picture of someone else's story.

Either way, your blueprint document becomes a great tool for you to be able to recall some of the moments in your life that you may have forgotten. You then have a chance to review those events with fresh eyes and derive new meaning that may not have been apparent in the past.

Lastly, I urge you to be kind to yourself as you review all the happenings in your blueprint as you will be digging up areas of your life that you may have been at war with in the past.

To continue on your road to owning your awesome, there is valuable feedback from your past that you should review with the intent of making progress and finding opportunities for self-improvement. Some of the patterns to look for and take note of in your blueprint as you reflect are as follows:

> You are not just the sum of your worst mistakes; you are so much more than that.

» Look for the times when you were happiest in your life.
» Notice what you were doing during those times that made you happy.
» Take note of any people, events, or activities that get you the most excited or give you the most satisfaction.
» Review each event and note which ones give you a stronger sense of self-esteem.
» Find any events that you can discuss with genuine enthusiasm without getting bored.

- » Review the times that you felt the most useful, the most needed and the most appreciated.
- » Take note of when you feel the best about yourself and your contributions.
- » Find and mark all the times that you felt best about yourself and your contributions.
- » Look for things that you may have forgotten about that made you feel especially good.

THE FEEDBACK RECEPTION TRAP

Like anything in life, feedback needs balance. More feedback is not necessarily always better. We talked earlier about the risks of an overload of information in the section about mentorship, but it also applies as you seek to gather simple and general feedback for yourself.

When you spend time asking too many people the same question you run the risk of getting yourself into a state of what I call analysis paralysis. That means you are in a continual state of gathering information and never take action because you have so much information to get through and decipher. Because of this you become confused and unable to figure out what the right move is for you.

One thing about feedback is that everyone tries to provide you with what they believe is good information as they see it. The trouble is not everyone sees the same things in the same way. Feedback is very subjective and too much of it will lead to conflicting opinions and leave you wondering who is right and who to trust.

People view things from their lens and from their experiences, and let's face it, we all have some hang-ups that can cloud our judgment. The one thing that I will caution you about in regard to feedback is to seek it only from people you trust so you know it will be accurate and trustworthy information.

Many of the people around us just want to be nice so they tell us what they think we want to hear, rather than actually what needs to be said. They choose kindness over truth with their advice, but that doesn't really do us any favors. It takes as much bold courage to give good feedback as well as it does to receive it.

3E PROCESS

Use the feedback you receive both from your own intuition (internal source) and also from external sources (other people) to become better prepared to own your awesome and live life on your terms.

Part of my secret to success in doing this lies within a process that I have used myself and shared with all of my clients. The process isn't difficult to understand and may even seem a little simplistic in nature. When it comes to self-improvement methods there is a beauty in simplicity. I assure you, despite its seeming simple this process packs a wallop for everyone with whom I have shared it.

The 3E process has three components just as the name implies. Consider it rather like three stages of self-improvement as you move through owning your awesome.

The first stage is you being actively engaged in your vision for the future, not just for today. When you are fully engaged in your future your vision becomes clear and you recognize that some changes need to happen and you are willing to do them. By purchasing this book and reading through it you have already shown the willingness to get fully engaged in being the master of owning your own awesome. Your internal feedback told you that you wanted something more from your life or your career or maybe both. Good for you for listening to your instinct and following your own feedback. First step, done - check!

The second component of the process to building lasting change and owning your awesome is to equip yourself with the tools you need to reach your goal. What I mean is, take the feedback from your blueprint, your own internal feedback, and gather it with the feedback from others. Then reflect on whether there are any gaps that are creating barriers preventing you from the journey or opportunities to be had. The barriers can often be seen in the fact that you may be lacking in skills, deficient in abilities, short on knowledge, or in need of assistance and cooperation from other people. Perhaps you are missing processes like the 3E process to help keep you on track and organized. Take time to review any possible options that could help close the gaps and get you on track to success.

The final stage in the process is for you to become empowered to make decisions. That means feeling confident as the decision maker and leader of your vision and taking action on the next steps. You can feel confident because you have done your homework by engaging in the right vision for you. You have equipped yourself by identifying all of the outstanding gaps, opportunities, and network needed to bring your vision to a reality.

The journey to owning your awesome is a trip filled with process improvement. Change is constant, so how you conduct and manage your time and focus as things change will make a huge difference in your results and success. The 3E process supports change and preempts crisis.

Discipline yourself to using these three steps regularly even when things seem to be going smoothly. Keep reviewing your goal to make sure it still makes sense to you, check on any new gaps or opportunities and make decisions and take action. By doing this you will always have a way to manage change, growth and impact.

> Change is constant, so how you conduct and manage your time and focus as things change will make a huge difference in your results and success.

THE STORY OF JILLIAN

A while back, I worked with a client who was looking for direction in her five-year-old business. She felt trapped and confused about where to go next with her planning. This client had realized a certain level of success, but her business was struggling and a bit cash poor as happens to many entrepreneurs.

She was having trouble connecting the dots to make a solid plan to bring in some paying clients who would also connect to the heart of who she was as a person. She was looking for her passion and some guidance to being a better leader to her team and her vision.

During our preliminary meeting, I discovered she was very unsure of herself and needed some self-esteem assistance and self-confidence about her ability to run her company. After much discussion that day, she left with the agreement to take on the challenge of the Time Capsule Blueprint exercise before we met again.

When we met for our second meeting she shared her experience with the exercise as being a major challenge for her, but also one that had a huge impact on her sense of who she was and where she wanted to go with her life and her business. The most memorable thing to come out of her experience with the blueprint was that she was unable to recall a time that she felt happy and powerful as the leader of her life. This was a significant moment of realization for her.

In her life there had been a lot of struggle and hardship through poverty and less than ideal relationships with others. It became even more apparent to her when it was down in black and white where she could take stock of her life. Those moments of discovery and quiet reflection became pivotal points for Jillian as she committed to changing her future story by improving her journey to owning her awesome.

Because of the exercise with the blueprint she was able to make decisions that day that changed her future and her life. She was careful not to fall into the trap of looking at her past with eyes of judgment, but instead with love and self-acceptance. She looked at her life in print with the sole purpose of finding and understanding opportunities for her own personal growth and improvement.

She didn't wallow in any self-doubt or self-deprecation about the results that were revealed, even though that could have been her natural tendency. I admired her that day because it took courage for her to see opportunity and goodness ahead.

In most cases people are so heavily programmed to see the negative in themselves it causes them grief as they try to forge ahead and move on. This wasn't the case for her, and I remember her saying she didn't want to blow her one shot at life so she was choosing to see opportunity and make changes to get into the journey of owning her awesome.

She wanted changes immediately and that is exactly what she did. From that day on Jillian embraced bold courage and walked her journey with intention. She continues today, nine years later with laser sharp focus on owning her awesome and creating the life she not only wanted but also the one she deserved.

For her, that included a solid business offering that sustained her lifestyle and left a legacy for her children.

Jillian is just one example of the power I have seen in the use of the Time Capsule Blueprint, but there are countless others. Today, many years later I am so pleased to say that Jillian owns a very successful business and travels the world teaching others her craft.

She practices bold courage every day and continually weighs her decisions and feedback against her dream of owning her awesome. This has made all the difference in her life. She is relentless in her pursuit of awesome and she rarely falters, but when she does she simply turns the page and moves on.

PART 5

LEADING THE SHIFT

CHAPTER 19

PREPARING TO LAUNCH

One of the amazing things about owning your awesome is that your definition and direction of awesome can and should change over time. Your awesome should never be considered finite. As you use the 3E process and gather feedback you will ebb, flow, learn and reflect on feelings and desires of what you want your awesome to look like.

The journey is constant and is ever changing like a river. Sometimes the river moves fast and furious, other times it is lazy and meandering. Sometimes it is wide and deep and other times it is narrow and shallow. The only thing constant about a river is change.

The same can be said for your journey to awesome. You may need to cross more than one kind of river to reach your destination, or fight some battles more than once.

My journey of owning my awesome certainly has had some fundamental shifts over the years. Some occurred as a result of feedback I had received from various individuals and other times I shifted out of sheer necessity using the 3E process to get back on course.

Chapter 19

A CASE FOR RESILIENCE

I remember a certain day so clearly because it was the moment I decided I needed an intervention or rather a reinvention of my life. I knew that it was going to take some bold courage to make it happen. I was in a very dark place and had just lived through some pretty harsh circumstances. In fact, I lost myself and the idea of owning any kind of awesome was hard to fathom since I was barely existing.

The thing about the need for reinvention is that it often requires a catalyst or a failure to make it happen. That is where my life was six months prior.

My adult life started as the typical story of a happy young newlywed which at that time for me was the ideal definition of owning my awesome. I had a husband I was crazy about, a beautiful son whom we both adored and a lovely home.

Although we weren't well off financially by any means, it was my storybook life.

We were happy until that fateful day when it all changed. What should have been an otherwise uneventful day turned into anything but.

The day started like thousands of others, where we got up, I put on the coffee and took care of our son while my beloved husband got ready for work. When the time came for my husband to leave for work, I kissed him as we said our goodbyes until he would return later that day.

We were happy with lots of excitement about the future and the family we were building. My husband was the general manager of a hotel and a well-respected man in the hospitality industry. He was the go-to guy for struggling hotels and resorts. He was regularly brought in to help get properties back on track in the business sense and operating smoothly. He was a professional businessman whom everybody loved.

I adored him.

Then it happened.

The morning he left for work I went about my normal day, which consisted of playing with my son and attending to his needs, preparing the meal for when my husband came home, and keeping my home tidy. I did what many other women did who had a new baby and a successful husband who could provide for our financial needs. It was my picture perfect life.

Then I got the call.

Six hours after I kissed my husband goodbye the phone rang while I was playing with our 10-month-old beautiful little boy. I answered the phone. On the other end of the line a woman I didn't recognize was screaming "Is your husband going to kill me, is he going to kill me?"

What?

I thought this must be a wrong number and said so.

"Paula, it's me, Kathy.

She worked on the front desk at the hotel where my husband was the manager.

"The police just told me he wants to kill me."

I was dumbfounded; at a complete loss. I thought this woman was out of her mind.

Is she referring to someone I know, I wondered. I didn't believe it when she said she meant my husband...that would have been ridiculous! The phone call made no sense to me.

At the same time there was a knock at the door and I was overcome with nausea.

I could see the flashing lights of a police cruiser in my driveway and right then my world started to slow down and everything seemed to be going in slow motion.

It was the kind of feeling where you know there are words and someone is talking but everything is suspended in time as you try with all your might to process the situation. That was me in that moment.

Chapter 19

There was a policeman at my door telling me that my husband had been locked in a psychiatric ward after he has threatened to kill three women and he was now in midst of a psychotic break.

I couldn't grasp what that meant at the time, but the officer asked me if he could provide me with a ride to the hospital.

I reeled in the feedback that the officers had given me, and my soul was shaken to the core.

In that moment of realization I understood that they were, in fact, talking about my beloved husband who had left only hours before as though everything had been normal.

It was so unbelievable to me that I could barely hear most of what they were saying. It was like my ears had a mind of their own and I felt deaf and could only see their mouths move, but I could not hear their words.

I couldn't breathe, my chest was tight and I stood there with shock exuding from my body.

That was the day my life turned upside down.

It was the most surreal moment of my life. We were the "in" couple. We lived an adventurous and glamorous life, living on big resorts and fine hotels. We travelled all the time to fancy places, dined like royalty and attended the best parties.

No one could have predicted my talented husband of four years and father to my young son would disappear in a split moment and never return.

My perfect family was vaporized and I was left with only memories and questions.

So many questions. As I looked at the police officer every ounce of my being didn't want to get in his car that day as I knew my life was never going to be the same.

My husband never returned home after that day. He was locked in a psychiatric ward under suicide watch and not able to function, oftentimes trapped in his mind with schizophrenic episodes and lapses of memory.

I was terrified, angry and sad all at the same time. Sometime later my darling husband was finally successful in his quest to end his own life.

But my life needed to continue.

From that moment on, life changed dramatically for my sweet baby boy and me. I went from being a happily married 26-year-old woman with a perfect life to suddenly being a single mother with a young baby and no source of income.

I kicked into survival mode and I was forced to make decisions for our immediate future. I very quickly had to move from my "perfect" bubble to the unknown, fending for myself and having to mature exponentially overnight.

I went from living in a beautiful home and enjoying the gift of being a stay at home mom with my son to being thrust back early into the workforce and eventually losing my home. I soon found myself living in a dirty, two-bedroom apartment in a not-so-likeable area of town. Nothing seemed easy.

I felt horribly alone and scared about what my life was becoming. Finances were so tight, I could barely afford to live. I lost my car because I couldn't afford the payments and was in serious danger of losing my home again. I was a mess with no solution in sight. I was receiving feedback from everywhere and everyone... some solicited, some not.

Most just sounded like noise, I couldn't really hear anything, as everything just seemed loud. My emotions got in the way of my being able to hear. That wasn't necessarily always a bad thing as everyone had an opinion during that time, and felt compelled to share what they thought I should or shouldn't be doing in that situation.

Everyone meant well, but I was over stimulated with so many people telling me how to be and what to do. Although I was gracious to thank them for their feedback, none of what they said mattered at the time.

Chapter 19

What I realized about their feedback was they had never been in my situation nor did they know what I was going through. My spirit was broken and I was quiet.

I found pleasure and solace in visiting with my parents. I visited often and they watched my son as I spent time alone in their pool. It was my quiet place where nobody told me how I should be and I could let go and try and hear myself think. Knowing my son was safe with my parents gave me some much needed time to breath and reflect on everything that had happened so far and allowed me time to think about what I was going to do to move forward.

During my time in the pool, I would dive under the water and scream with all my might. When I ran out of air I would come to the surface and draw in another deep breath, sink back down and scream again. I did this over and over until I became exhausted and had released what I could that day. There was something incredibly therapeutic about being in the silence of the water with the sunlight streaming above and nothing to hear except my own voice. I carried out this routine for the next three months.

During that time I also did a lot of thinking and a lot of healing. I reflected on everything, and I pretty much had my own state of the union address right there in my parent's backyard each day. I thought about what I had lost, what I still had, and what I longed for in the future. At times, it was confusing because it was hard to move beyond my past as well as the challenges and pain of the present to even dream about the future.

Despite that, I realized that even in the midst of feeling afraid I would have to go ahead and do things anyway in order to make change. This situation was no different. I was afraid and I had no idea how to start tackling my situation and turning it around, but I decided that I was willing to try.

All of those pool sessions were helping me to heal and renewing my hope and faith in life as well. On my last bob that day I came up and broke the surface of the water and knew that whether I was afraid or not I had to change my life and regain my sense of owning my awesome.

I made it through my time of grieving and was ready to forge ahead for something brighter and happier. Many people share their dramatic story of how something happened and suddenly they are saved and everything becomes simple and they live happily ever after. While that may be true for some, I believe my story is closer to what most people experience.

I made the decision for improvement. Period. I was not going to allow myself to live that way in the depths of despair. At that point my life owned me and was giving me a run for my money, rather than me owning my awesome. I was determined to switch that dynamic.

Still, nothing was simple and there was no magic button to get where I wanted to go, but I had rediscovered my self-determination and my warrior spirit was coming back. I knew that owning my awesome would take time and practice and it definitely wasn't something that would come overnight.

During the process, I had slip-ups and fearful moments where I risked slipping back into my darkness, but I found the strength to get back up and keep going. The fact that I slipped wasn't really a big deal. The important part was that I no longer lived in the darkness, I would make the decision to pull myself back to life and out of those negative thought patterns, even if I momentarily slipped.

The feedback still came my way from every source imaginable, but because of my decision to own my awesome, I was better able to manage it. During my time in the pool, I realized that the most important feedback that I needed to hear and get control of was my own. I had become my own worst enemy in a sense that I was angry at myself for failing in my marriage, failing financially, failing as a mother and simply not feeling smart enough to move through this quicker. None of this had any basis in reality, but still I was tormented.

Chapter 19

I chastised myself harshly all the time. I told myself I should have been better at managing my life. Yet, here I was with no husband, no career, in debt and with a young son who needed me. I had a lot of "if only" moments that I deliberated on, such as, "if only I was a better wife, a smarter woman, more skilled, etc." That kind of thinking wasn't helpful and in fact, it was hurtful and slowed my progress to owning my awesome.

Once I realized my internal feedback to myself was actually hurting me more than encouraging me, I was determined to change my story for myself and for my family's future. I had to be resilient and diligent about watching my thoughts and my actions towards myself. I became vigilant about protecting myself from my own thoughts.

I focused on being kind to myself and offering as much grace as I would have given someone else in that situation. Remember there were two sets of rules. One set of standards I held for me and one set I held for others. It was time I bridged that gap before I let my internal feedback ruin my life. I set forth on my new adventure that day.

PART 5

LEADING THE SHIFT

CHAPTER 20

THE ART OF WINNING

Self-talk is feedback to yourself. Most times it takes the form of criticism rather than positive affirming thoughts. I know mine was.

My self-talk was filled with guilt, sarcasm, self-loathing, general put downs and sheer cruelty. I rarely gave myself any resemblance of a kind word. It was painful all the time.

Despite that I was generally a happy, positive person. I gave others grace even if they didn't deserve it, I found a place in my heart to forgive easily. I could see past flaws that a person had and love them unconditionally.

Nonetheless, if my internal dialogue to myself at that time could have been overheard by anybody, it would have been considered abuse to myself. A stranger hearing another person speaking to me as I spoke to myself would have likely stepped forward to defend me from such harsh judgments. I gave myself no grace and no kindness. If self-loathing were an Olympic sport, I would have won the gold medal. That needed to stop if I was going to own my awesome.

Chapter 20

You get good at what you practice. I had spent six months quietly becoming a specialist in berating myself. I was now quite adept and skilled at it, and that wasn't something I was proud of.

Internal feedback can be tough to overcome because it is stronger, more direct and more difficult to dismiss than other forms of feedback. It can be incredibly difficult to dismiss your own thoughts. However, if I can do it (and I did), so can you. I needed to learn a new skill so I could stop that negative habit in its tracks. It has since become a life-long discipline to manage my inner voice and make sure it is used for my own good.

PRACTICE MAKES PERFECT

Within just a matter of months and some hard, focused work on my own self-talk, my overall well-being in all areas of my life started to shift to a new season of hope and action. I became a fighter for my own prosperity and my dream life. I worked and did whatever it took to embrace the life that was handed to me and turn it into the life I desired.

I was determined to own my awesome despite the hand I had been dealt, so I took action. I started applying for new jobs and finally landed one that afforded me decent pay and hours that fit with being a single mother. I was thrilled! I was working in a high school with special needs students teaching life skills and vocational skills and I loved it. It was work that connected with my spirit and I was excited to serve the teenagers every day. From the students to my colleagues, it was a wonderful time for me of feeling like I had purpose. Joy was coming back into my life.

I was steadily getting back on track with my finances and feeling some sense of security with my newly created situation. I was starting to own my awesome again and I loved it! Unfortunately, less than six months after I started that job, the government announced the cutback of 40,000 jobs within the education sector and my job was one of the casualties.

This was a prime opportunity for my negative self-talk to kick into high gear again and for me to start to berate myself for not seeing the job loss coming, but I didn't fall into that trap. Instead, I remained intentional about what I wanted and how I was going to continue to own more of my awesome going forward. Rather than curling into a ball and feeling overwhelmed with another blow, I forced myself to dream about what the possibilities could be.

I had four months before the end of the school year to figure out what I was going to do. I gave my all to finding a solution and being proactive about my situation. The new me was someone who wanted to create some sense of security for myself and my son and to do that I needed to stay focused. I needed to complete my mission without allowing myself to derail and fall into the perils of my own disappointment. I liked who I was becoming very much.

Driving to work one day shortly after hearing the news about my impending job loss, I listened to the news on the radio. The newscaster was sharing the plight of the teachers, non-profit organizations and families who were affected by the impending cutbacks. He was sharing my plight. What came next was a pure coincidence and a thing of beauty all at the same time. Right after the radio announcer discussed my job loss story, he announced that funding was being cut dramatically for all non-profit organizations and the services currently available in the city were going to be affected in a big way.

Some of the agencies receiving cuts were the ones that served the same population of young adults who were graduating from high school and would be needing placement for housing, employment and/or rehabilitation day programming services. Because of the cuts, the already lengthy waiting lists would rise to record levels. The parents were exasperated because their long term care plans for the children were crumbling in front of them and they had very few options left.

Chapter 20

The wheels started to turn in my head. I've always said that opportunity doesn't come with directions. Sometimes we need to jump out of the proverbial plane and learn how to assemble our parachute on the way down. My brain was firing on all cylinders after that newscast. I pieced together information that I heard. I started to get excited.

I saw the possibility for me to start some kind of business that would assist all of these people who would no longer have access to the government services they needed. My internal messages were screaming at me that I could figure this out! Knowledge is an amazing thing and when I started to become more attuned to grabbing feedback and information from a variety of areas (including myself), my wisdom and innovation increased.

There is nothing more empowering than gathering knowledge and having the ability to piece things together for a solution to any problem. Feedback in this case brought clarity and enabled me to make plans and decisions that were informed and hopeful about my future.

I found myself energized, even in the face of adversity. It was almost like I said, "challenge accepted." I was ready to take on whatever I needed to do to find a solution. I felt powerful, and I was powerful. I now knew I had the tenacity of spirit that would make me unstoppable in pursuit of my goals. I dared to dream of a new future and was willing to ask of myself, "what else is possible?"

I realized I needed a plan of action for the next steps. I started talking to parents of the kids that I was currently working with. I worked with high school aged students with cognitive and physical disabilities. Although they were in a high school, their programming was customized, based on their abilities and level of comprehension. The high school was large with more than 2,000 students attending daily. It also had the luxury of a dedicated state of the art developmental center where an additional seventy students who had varying degrees of disabilities attended.

As the parents heard the news they immediately panicked and asked me for my feedback on what I thought they should do. Rather than answer quickly, I started asking them questions like "What if I got a location, hired trained staff and created an engaging day program? Would you consider signing a one-year contract for the care of your child?"

Through those conversations I gained more and more feedback and my idea was born. I was delighted by their resounding yesses! Parent after parent agreed and in just a few short weeks I had my first sixteen signed annual contracts. I was officially on my way to starting my first company.

I assessed the sheer scope of the business I was formulating in my head and I realized I needed help to run it. I found a business partner who wanted to commit and help. I had a line of credit of $10,000 which I drained to invest into getting the company going. I opened the first fee for service social service agency in Canada serving developmentally challenged teens and adults and individuals living with an acquired brain injury.

We opened our doors that fall and took in our first clients. I was excited and afraid and, make no mistake, as I went through this process I had plenty of internal turmoil and days that were more doubtful than others. But I pushed through and focused on the positive and the possibilities. I was intentionally grateful for my journey and by doing that it helped me to ward off any negative messages that came my way.

The external feedback coming from parents and the buzz within our community brought a level of credibility to my new business. We gained a lot of great attention in the media, and we became respected as a viable and highly sought after service option.

We quickly gained referrals and partnership opportunities from other non-profits as well as from the City of London. I was named Entrepreneur of the Year that year and was featured in a number of magazines across Canada. Our business grew to three cities and 27 employees within a matter of 36 months. It was exhilarating!

I had purpose, was fueling my new passion for entrepreneurship and was doing life successfully on my own – and I was better than okay. I was owning my awesome. I loved who I was becoming. I became a person of big ideas, but also a person of incredible skill able to pull ideas together and bring them to fruition. I beamed with pride.

FIND YOUR FEEDBACK FILTER

I realized I hadn't beamed with pride since before my husband had experienced his mental breakdown. It felt so good to feel positive and alive again with possibilities.

When my husband was overcome by his mental illness, I fell into a darkness of my own. It was not one of mental illness but I was buried in feedback and advice from every direction. Everyone else's thoughts were so loud in my head that I couldn't filter out what I really needed to hear. The challenge for me was to hear my own internal feedback and change it. Learning to trust my intuition while filtering through the feedback I got from others was crucial to my success or failure.

Many times our biggest barriers to success are ourselves because the things we tell ourselves limit us. I didn't want to live behind my own limiting beliefs anymore. I was dealt a situation in life that was painful for certain, but I didn't want that event to define how or what my future looked like. In fact, the most important part of that story with my husband is for you to remember the lesson of resiliency. Once I changed my attitude that things were possible, I had the power to change my own life. You can do it too. I am not saying it will be easy, since changing our own bad habits and being accountable to ourselves is difficult. But I am telling you it will be worth it.

Changing the way I managed and saw myself and my situation changed my life. In order to do that, I had to filter the feedback I was receiving. The most important focus for me was my own feedback. My life was forever changed that day with my husband's breakdown, but change is imminent for everyone. What matters is what you do with the change.

PART 5

LEADING THE SHIFT

CHAPTER 21

RELATIONSHIPS MATTER

Whether you are aware of it or not, you have been giving feedback to those around you for as long as you have been in a relationship with them.

From the very first time you see a person across the room or utter your first word in an introductory email, you are generating some form of feedback.

Feedback in form of communication. Communication is critical to every good relationship, whether it is with friends, co-workers, your children or your spouse. The foundation from which you build a relationship with someone is based solely on how you communicate and give feedback to each other.

When there is little or no communication, there is generally a weak relationship. Even deciding whether you will communicate rarely or frequently with someone is in itself a form of feedback to them.

When we make an effort and communicate effectively we are showing respect for what the other person thinks and means to us. We typically share freely of ourselves to those with whom we want stronger relationships.

When we communicate with others we generally have a goal in mind. Sometimes we communicate to persuade people to our point of view. We help them see the light to a problem or situation. We also communicate to provide and seek information.

Feedback from others is how we garner our information about them, about their feelings and how their minds work. We also communicate to express our emotions and indicate our favor and appreciation for events or gestures.

To communicate with others we use three basic methods: verbal (spoken), written, and non-verbal (our body language). It is important to recognize that we don't have to speak or write anything to be giving feedback to others. Our message is apparent on our face or expressed through our gestures. Our body language tells people things we may not even wish to say, but which are impossible to hide. For example, we may have a distaste for someone or something and our body language gives it away even though we haven't said anything. Our body language is most apparent and readable by those with whom we spend a lot of time.

FAMILIAR RULES OF CONDUCT

Everyone who currently has a place in your life has a set of rules of conduct they follow when they are around you. They know what to expect from you and how to act appropriately in that current situation. From experience and the feedback you give they know how to please you (and displease you) and relate to you and there is comfort in that for both of you.

You have acted and interacted in a consistent way with them for whatever period of time you've been in a relationship with them and that is what they expect going forward. When you are predictable in your behavior, the people you love and are close to have a benchmark. That is a level of expectation about how you will respond. Everyone does their best to work within those confines, ensuring harmony with you as best they can. This is a healthy occurrence and helps relationships to grow stronger and flourish.

In most situations people develop an expectation of what to expect in their various relationships. When something is amiss or changes with one of the parties and the other isn't aware of it, that is when confusion and conflict occur. When someone makes changes without good communication there is often misunderstanding and friction and relationships risk breakdown.

Embracing bold courage and the journey to owning your awesome will change you and you will start to see things differently. You will make changes to how you do things, what you expect from others and what you want from your relationships in order to achieve your desired life. This is normal. It is all part of figuring out who you are, who you want to become and how you want to live your life going forward.

Consider change as an influx of positive news on your personal reinvention journey because it means you are moving forward. Change is critical and allows momentum, helping you get to the point where you feel like you are living and owning your awesome. During the process, change will become the norm for you. It fact, it will be expected.

But if you do not give your community of people proper feedback about these changes that you are experiencing, you will experience problems in your relationships. It is important to note that you are under no obligation to be the person you were a year, a month ago or even 15 minutes ago. However, to have healthy and joyful relationships with those you love, you are under an obligation to notify them of the changes.

RISK OF CULTURE SHOCK

Culture shock is real and it is strong, and it is generally tied to when you move to a new environment that is different from what you are used to. It happens when you are immersed in a new culture or when expectations change in your old culture.

I encourage you to be aware that as you move forward taking on new experiences you will change swiftly. During this time of change you risk creating culture shock for those who care about you. They may not understand why you are becoming bolder and more outgoing.

Their culture shock comes from the fact that the relationships around them are changing because you are and you haven't shared your news. They don't have any warning and they cannot see the changing landscape as it is being thrust on them without any notice. After all, you have a history together of being and interacting a certain way. If that suddenly needs to change for you to own your awesome, you need to give them grace.

When your behavior changes, as it often will when you truly start to own your awesome, those around you become perplexed and often don't understand what is going on. This leads to hurt feelings and insecurity in the relationship. They may become bewildered, disoriented as to where they fit in with this new way of being. With confusion and emotions running high they then become unclear on how to fix the situation. The truth is they can't fix what they don't understand. It is your job to help them and to find ways to provide them with the proper feedback so they can explain the changes they are seeing. You can also share your need for support as you transition into your new way of living.

The transition will be much smoother and more pleasant if you can get your people on board. By giving them feedback and reassurance you are giving them new instructions and a new set of rules of engagement for interaction with you and what is expected going forward. For some people in your life, this may mean big changes and for others it may mean very little. For some it will be exciting for them as they may have been waiting for you to fly.

As you grow into your new reality of who you want to be and own your awesome, don't make hasty decisions that you may regret. Give people a chance to get on board with you and be patient if they are nervous and falter during the changes. Remember that you likely mean a lot to them and they will fear being forgotten or even losing you from their lives when they see drastic change occurring.

If the relationship is worth having and is an important part of your life, then it will be worth it for you to take the time with the other person and allow them to catch up to you in thought and understanding. If they were your cheerleaders and confidants before, there is no reason to expect they won't still support you as you go forward into this new territory of owning your awesome.

SOLO CONVERSATIONS

It is so easy to get so caught up in the planning of your journey and your new life that you forget to bring other important people into the fray and allow them time to acclimatize to the new environment. It's understandable that as you get excited, you want progress right away and expect everyone to jump into the deep end of the pool with you. It is easy to forget that you waded into your pool of change by entering via the shallow end and have had time to get accustomed to your new way of thinking and acting.

Your loved ones, on the other hand, haven't had that luxury of being eased into the pool and that isn't their fault. If you make changes without adequately providing feedback to them, it is the equivalent of throwing them in the deep end with all their clothes on. That is shocking for everyone.

Let them into your thoughts and then give them time to catch up to you in their understanding and acceptance. They will come alongside and support you if the relationship you have is based on mutual respect, love and trust. If they don't catch up and refuse to make any changes for you, then it may be time to reconsider that particular relationship.

I am very prone to having full conversations with myself, making plans and decisions and then expecting everyone to know what I am thinking. I forget to share, and then I get frustrated with those around me if they aren't up to speed with me. The kicker is, it isn't their fault, and I have no right to get upset because I literally have neglected to share any of what I am thinking. If only I had taken the time to share with them, we could all have gotten on board together and the frustrations would have been avoided.

However, I am in my head a lot with my thoughts and I have full and thorough conversations with myself about my ideas, but then forget to share it all with others. Because of that, those around me also get very discouraged.

I have great people around me and we all try to do whatever we can to support and help each other, but when the communication breaks down it is sometimes very difficult. Typically when friction hits I realize that I have forgotten to provide others with feedback to my progress or new thoughts and they are in complete misunderstanding of what I am trying to do. In my haste and excitement I try to skip steps in the journey and it rarely works.

If I want people to come along on my journey, I need to prepare them and allow a certain amount of time to get them acclimatized to my plan. You will need to do this too. Throwing people into the deep end with all their clothes on and then not understanding why they are upset doesn't get anyone very far.

I know now that it is a much smoother journey to owning my awesome if instead I invite them into the pool with me by sharing my dreams, hopes and thoughts for my future. I extend my hand to guide them to where I am and most every time they will trust me and take it.

PART 6

PUTTING IT ALL TOGETHER

CHAPTER 22

CONNECTING THE DOTS

The second best thing that can happen to a person or a company is that through their efforts they connect the dots and find success at what they are trying to achieve. This success may include personal growth, skill attainment, leadership acumen, increased revenues, decreased expenses and improved relationships among other benefits. Success almost always feels good. I think we can all agree that attaining success is a wonderful thing and a major motivator for everyone.

Contrary to popular belief, however, success doesn't always breed success unless you know how it happened.

The first and absolute best thing that can happen to a person or company is that through their efforts they connect the dots and create success that they can duplicate. When successful outcomes can be replicated, that is when the magic happens for the organization and massive growth can occur. The same is true in your life.

Duplication of success is extremely difficult without having a standard process or formula to follow. When trial and error are used in the quest for success and no records are kept or a system isn't developed, the success will often occur by coincidence or through a stroke of good luck. While the immediate success feels great, the reality of the situation is that to achieve long term success and reduce day to day stress, you will benefit greatly from implementing a process for success. It needs to be easy to use and see results from.

By not implementing a more solid system for success you run the risk of your luck eventually failing and your level of fatigue and stress rising as you continue to try and reinvent the wheel and to live life the way you've always done it. There will come a point when this wears thin and your level of success becomes more difficult to sustain.

Such is the case with start-up companies. Teams race quickly to progress and try new things without ever taking stock of what is working. They do not create a blueprint so they can duplicate their smart efforts for success, and as a result, they burnout after only a few years.

Many of the top companies in the world are process centric. They build and work on a model of continuous process improvement and innovation to better optimize their efforts for continued success and to attempt to hold onto that sweet spot at the top of the consumer market.

Because I firmly believe in process, many of the clients that I have advised over the years also create a process centric culture and they regard almost like their insurance policy for success. They create a standard mode of conduct for all activities within their organization so that no matter who is doing the activity, the steps and outcomes are identical. They literally turn everything they do into an opportunity for improvement in order to further their agenda.

I love working with these types of clients as there is always a base line from which to start and it is easy to measure impact when we are making changes and decide whether those changes are leading them in the right direction. My favorite thing about process, other than the ability to duplicate success, is the ability to ask questions along the way. We can clearly see if what we want to have happen is actually happening.

When we work within a process it is much easier to ensure that our actions are consistent, aligned and repeatable with the outcomes we are hoping for. When you have consistency, alignment and repeatability, you have the makings of a successful process and a positive outcome.

I have helped thousands of organizations build, formulate and monitor their processes. I have also assisted executives looking for better ways to manage their own leadership capabilities and how they deal more effectively and efficiently in their day to day life.

The same theory and relative importance of process holds true for you individually while on your personal journey to owning your awesome. It is really easy to say you have bold courage. However, when faced with debilitating fears and uncertainty about the present and the future, it is so much easier to tackle the process of managing change and growth by having a system to follow.

Through my years of research and in building trusted relationships with my clients, it is clear to me that when people are given a framework for daily management of their work and lives, it also gives them a vision and allows for accountability. As a result of that, their level of success rose significantly.

Those same people were also able to consistently replicate the success they were creating over and over again, thus reducing their stress and increasing their quality of satisfaction. By replicating successful outcomes, it becomes easier for everyone to stay engaged in the process and stay motivated towards those outcomes. It allows for a faster road to success. Having a process is also a vital system to lean on when stress is high and times are more challenging. The process helps you figure out the solution to any problem, thus saving time, energy and further mental and emotional drain.

By implementing a system for successfully tracking intended outcomes, your journey can be faster, easier and more enjoyable. You will be more consistently aligned with your goal of owning your awesome and have a strategy to achieve that success every single day.

PUTTING THE AWE BACK IN YOUR AWESOME

Awesome is one of the most overused words in the English speaking language today. You will even find campaigns enlisting members to help stamp out the word awesome from our language. You will find hundreds of lists of suggested alternatives to substitute for the word awesome in order to stop using the word entirely. Because of the overuse of the word awesome, it has lost its power and its true meaning.

In the beginning the word awesome meant causing feelings of fear or wonder. From there, it morphed into a superlative that meant overall greatness, magnificence and outstanding. Today, it's used commonly as a generally positive descriptor like "great", "cool" or even just "okay." It seems that everything is awesome these days. "That carpet looks awesome" "Buddy, your spoon collection is awesome" "My, sweetie, you look awesome" "Hey bro, your tattoo is awesome."

The word has lost its oomph and is used to describe everything from the quality of your lunch to the color match of shoes to your pants. Your lunch may have only been entirely adequate, yet you have a tendency to say it was awesome...the same for the shoes and pants color match.

While I agree the word in many cases is overused and has lost some of the power of its glory days, I don't believe we should stop using it altogether. It's a good word! Rather than ditch the word altogether I have found a way to put the punch back into it. So when you own your awesome, you will put the true AWE back into the word awesome. Once again, it will reign supreme as the greatest descriptor of all time. You will live an awe-filled lifestyle, not one that is just entirely adequate like your lunch. It will be a great tasting juicy life and it deserves a proper descriptor.

When you speak of your life you will have earned the right to use the word awesome in all of its glory. It truly will mean awe inspired and be superlative. Your life will be everything and more that you have wanted it to be – it truly will be AWESOME.

Chapter 22

A NEW SYSTEM FOR SUCCESS

To help you put the AWE back into your awesome there are a few steps you can take.

I recommend consistent use of the Success Tracker System, a process I devised after working with thousands of different clients and watching them struggle to bolster their self-confidence and lead their vision.

Most people love simplicity and progress. The Success Tracker System is simple and is able to show your progress as you move through your journey to owning your awesome. The process itself helps keep you on track and increases your chances of success. The results revealed from the use of the process have been fantastic. In fact, they are even better than I thought they might be.

When my clients used the process, they were better able to track their progress, stay aligned to their goals, see incremental success and enjoy the fruits of their effort. As all of that occurred, their personal satisfaction increased substantially and their confidence soared, creating a perfect scenario for them to be motivated to continue their journey.

The process also provides some instant gratification in that you can measure if the decisions you are making match your intended actions, words and emotions required to live and own you're awesome. It becomes easier to recognize if what you want to have happen is actually happening. Each decision, action, and step forward that you make with bold courage is one step closer to putting that AWE into your awesome.

When you use the system it doesn't matter whether you are using the process to reshape and renew your business goals or if you are working on personal issues. The system is proven to have great positive impact on both. It provides the framework for daily management as you make decisions and decide relevance to your outcome, clarify satisfaction and ensure alignment.

The Success Tracker System is a six-step process that, when used consistently, will enhance your own personal leadership effectiveness, assist in process improvement and serve as a change management solution that can also improve business outcomes. When you use this system you become more empowered and your uncertainty and lack of self-confidence are reduced. Clarity brings targeted action and targeted action brings successful results. When you use this process repeatedly your success can be replicated over and over again.

I recommend that you take the Success Tracker System and implement it into your daily life of owning your awesome. You will enjoy the structure and the rewards.

PART 6

PUTTING IT ALL TOGETHER

CHAPTER 23

THE SUCCESS TRACKER SYSTEM

In your current state of living you may or may not feel or think of yourself as a leader, but you are – we all are.

You truly are the leader of your own life and it is up to you to make the choice to own that role and be more intentional in what you will do with it and how you lead yourself.

It is also up to you to choose how you will impact and lead others around you. That all starts with accepting the title of leader and deciding to own your awesome!

As a leader you can sometimes find yourself stuck, unable to reach that level of fulfillment you dream of. Then one day you make the simple decision to make the leap with bold courage and embark on owning your awesome.

The Success Tracker System was created as a tool to engage, equip and empower you to realize your results of owning your awesome in a more seamless and smarter way. As you become more conscious of how you live and work, you will be able to make more educated decisions that are aligned with your larger vision of owning your awesome. Simply put, your awesome is your fulfilled life – your way – everyday.

The Success Tracker System is a process tool to enable you to get better focused and more organized so that you can lead yourself and others more productively. Consider it a catalyst for results. By committing to it, you will unleash your desire to own your awesome in a more intentional way.

Here is how it works.

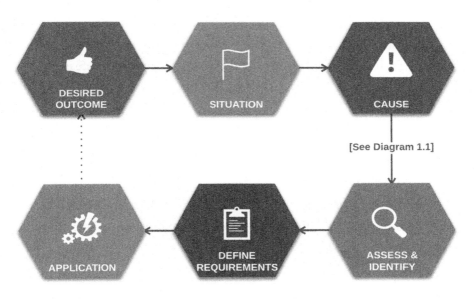

Diagram 1.0 The Success Tracker System

STEP 1 – DEFINE YOUR OUTCOME

The first step in using the system is to define your intended outcome. The Success Tracker System focuses on one intended outcome at a time. You may have more than one outcome in motion at a time depending on what you would like to accomplish.

Chapter 23

At this point in your journey you will have already completed this first step by defining what owning your awesome looks like in your mind. For example, you may wish to be have a financially stronger business (your awesome) and the steps to perhaps make that happen are 1) increased sales 2) increased client touch points 3) better expense control or decrease in non-essential spending. Those 3 things would be considered your key performance indicators or sub segments – meaning those items that you use as a benchmark for progress and if you successfully improve them, it will directly affect your desired larger outcome.

This system will help you stay consistent, aligned and repetitive with your actions, your words and your emotions to get results and achieve your optimal state of fulfillment and satisfaction in the process.

Defining intended outcomes or areas of growth for all areas of your work and life is a smart strategy to realize results time and time again. When you do this it allows you to get focused and commit to those areas in which you want to achieve excellence or success and that require your attention now.

The journey to owning your awesome is just that, a journey, and with daily actions and the building of good habits your potential for success increases dramatically.

Consider owning your awesome as your personal mission for excellence, a challenge to increase your potential in the important areas of your life. These segments typically include personal and spiritual growth, physical environment, fun and recreation, business and career, money, health, friends and family, and love and romance.

In the case of bold courage, keep your chosen segments top of mind as the larger overarching categories for improvement.

I believe that each individual must find a desired rhythm for their life that makes sense for them and enables them to own their awesome. Prioritize and focus your attention on those chosen segments that are important to your journey right now.

For example, one of the segments I chose to focus on was to increase success in my business. To identify the most important outcomes I wanted to achieve, I divided the business segment into smaller sections.

One of the keys to using this process to its maximum is to understand that there are numerous sub-segments that you can focus on within each larger segment. For example, in relation to leading better business operations I could have chosen smaller sections such as administration, technology, human resources or marketing.

At that particular time, I made it a priority to focus on sales development. As I broke the sales development subsection down into smaller pieces I was better able to make a plan based on incremental goals. Bold Courage gets you working on things that fuel your passion and when passion is ignited, stuff gets done!

The same was true with my health. I might have a large goal to run a triathlon but first I must achieve and realize success in a more attainable physical challenge. The truth is at the time, I wasn't very fit. The gap between my desired physical state and my actual physical state was large, so recognizing that I needed to start with incremental goals was important.

Once you decide on your intended outcome there will be opportunities to break that outcomes down into similar bite sized morsels. As you do that, they are easier to manage, track and see progress. Planning the goals helps you to see quick progress, lead more productively and efficiently, and keeps you motivated to keep going.

> Bold Courage gets you working on things that fuel your passion and when passion is ignited, stuff gets done!

The beauty of the Success Tracker System is that no matter the depth or breadth of the intended outcome you wish to achieve, the process remains the same. You can safely, assuredly and effectively use the system to build consistency, alignment and repeatability for your success in all segments of your life.

STEP 2 – DEFINE THE CURRENT SITUATION

Define your current situation as it relates to your intended outcome. The reality of your current situation is important so you can see the difference between where you want to get to versus where you are now. You will use this information to make judgment calls and future decisions further along in this process. This is the benchmark from which you will start your planning.

STEP 3 – IDENTIFY THE CAUSE OF THE CURRENT SITUATION

You'll need to be honest and take a solid look at the root cause of your current situation. Stubborn and recurrent problems are often symptoms of deeper issues. Honesty with yourself in identifying the root cause is the only way you are going to be able to improve your situation. Take care to drill down and get to the underlying cause of the issue as this is the answer to why the disruption is happening.

Only when you reach the root cause can you make the proper decisions and set forth plans to improve the situation. In much the same way as a doctor wants to treat the cause of an illness rather than simply treating the symptoms, you too must go back to the primary cause. Like the doctor, if you only treat the symptoms of your problem you will never be able to achieve true sustainable improvement in the situation.

There are many different methods to find the root cause of an issue available to you, but my favorite and the one I recommend to most of my clients is the "5 why" method.

I like it because it is a simple and thorough technique that you can use to quickly get to the root of the situation. It is also a multipurpose method that can be used when your process isn't working properly and you aren't attaining the desired results.

When we fail to ask the right questions and go deep enough into why our efforts aren't working, it throws the balance of the process out of alignment. When the process is out of alignment, the results will vary. When results vary, you should go back to the root cause step and ask why and push a little further to find the true root cause.

The way to use the "5 why" method is to ask why until you reach the root cause. Asking why five times is generally a good rule of thumb, but you may reach the answer a little sooner or a little later depending on the situation. As you ask why and develop your answers, make sure your answers are grounded in fact and not in feeling. Then ask why again. Continue in this manner until you reach the point where you have defined the root cause.

Once you feel confident that you have gotten down to the underlying cause of the situation you are ready to move into the next step in the process.

STEP 4 – ASSESSMENT AND DEVELOPMENT OF OPTIONS

Once the root cause of your situation has been clearly identified, you will want to assess and identify what your options are to change that situation and make improvements towards your intended outcome. The best way to do that is through the use of the SOME™ analysis.

The SOME™ analysis is one I developed specifically in reference to owning your awesome, but it works well in any problem solving opportunity when used in conjunction with the Success Tracker System six-step process.

SOME™ is an acronym for Solutions, Opportunities, Mindset and External Factors.

This analysis is used to assess four factors in relation to your situation. The acronym will make it easy for you to remember as you try to break down the cause and assess and identify "some" options for improvement.

Through this analysis you will look at all options, both internal and external for improvement in your situation

Basically, a SOME™ analysis helps you determine how all four of these factors will affect the performance and activities of owning your awesome in the long-term. The SOME™ analysis is often used in collaboration with other analytical business tools like the 5 Why's and the AWE™ principle to give a clear understanding of a situation and related internal and external factors.

Before you jump ahead and start using this analysis, you should understand it completely and be aware of what each of the factors signifies.

SOLUTIONS

The first element is solutions. Look at your situation and what you have within yourself right now that could solve the problem. Ask yourself: What can I do right now to better my situation and cause?

Some things to consider as you answer this question are the skills, abilities, knowledge and subject matter expertise that you currently possess. All of them could help change your situation. Make a list of all of those items. In doing that, you may find you already have the solution at your fingertips to bring improvement to the situation.

OPPORTUNITIES

The second element is Opportunities. Make a list of opportunities outside of your own self and capabilities that could assist in the improvement of your intended outcome. These opportunities may be through other people in your network, available funding, accessible information and education you could attain, to name a few. You may have other external opportunities in your life that are also available to you and worthwhile for you to review as a means of impacting the solution.

MINDSET

Your mindset throughout this entire process is paramount and worth noting. Your mindset is your way of thinking. It is the mental attitude that predetermines your responses to your situation. Mindset is the third element in the SOME™ principle and is quick and easy to notate.

Simply list what your current mindset is in relation to the situation you are trying to improve. Make a list of three or four adjectives that describe your current emotional state. Depending on the situation, your adjectives may be positive or negative. What matters is that you are aware of them and that you document your mindset. Set that list aside in a safe place for now.

EXTERNAL FACTORS

Once you have assessed and identified the solutions, opportunities and mindset you must look at any external factors that could affect your situation. The last element to review in the SOME™ principle is external factors.

External factors are defined as those circumstances or facts that are beyond your control that could affect your plan of owning your awesome. Some of these external factors could be, but aren't limited to, environment, legal issues, gaps in product, threats, safety regulations and foreign exchange rates. For example, if one of your intended outcomes involves a greater profit margin on your product and you import your product from a foreign country, one of the external factors that you could be facing is the foreign exchange rate disrupting your healthy mark up.

STEP 5 – DEFINE YOUR REQUIREMENTS

In any process there is always a point where you need to define requirements to better support you along the way. This is where you can set forth a plan to make improvements towards your desired outcome to better own your awesome.

There are four key categories that are used in this process improvement exercise.

- **Commitment** – Make a list of all the commitments you will set forth and conquer to improve this situation. The more the commitments are specific, measurable, achievable, realistic and timely, the better your success will be.
- **Recognition** – Define what you need to take into consideration or be aware of in your effort to improve the situation. This will be helpful in furthering your decision-making process and having realistic expectations of time frames.
- **Satisfaction** – This is a simple, yet critical component to this process. Ask yourself the very important question: "By completing this plan of action (commitments made), will this increase my satisfaction?" You need to answer only yes or no. If the answer is yes, then proceed and identify at least one thing you can show gratitude for as your situation is improved. If the answer is no, then that is a clear sign that this piece of the puzzle to owning your awesome is not relevant to the overall journey. When things aren't relevant, don't waste time on them.
- **Feedback** – Review your plan of commitment and see what information or feedback would assist you along the way. Then make plans to gather the desired information. The easier you can make your path to completing your commitments, the better it is. You will be more motivated and things won't seem so overwhelming.

STEP 6 – APPLICATION

The secret sauce to having bold courage is having positive and hopeful perspective. Perspective is your mental view of a situation. How you see a situation has direct impact on your mindset. Your mindset affects your performance or your ability to execute a task successfully.

In the Success Tracker System the key performance indicators for your performance and ultimately your success is based in AWE. This is the golden jewel of bold courage and where we put the awe back into awesome. AWE is an acronym for your actions, words and emotions. In order to put the awe back into your awesome, you should strive to have your actions, words and emotions match your optimal mindset. When you do this, success will come easier and you will truly have that feeling of awe in the best sense of the word.

Awe is defined as:

Actions: The way in which you conduct yourself towards you and others.

Words: The way in which you speak to others and the words you use in your internal dialogue with yourself.

Emotions: The strong feeling derived from your circumstance, mood or relationship with others.

The first piece in this part of the process is to define your optimal mindset. To do that you should review your commitments (from the previous step) and your desired outcomes. As you do that, write down the best descriptor of a mindset anyone could have in that situation to achieve success. Define what the ideal picture of mindset looks like (whether you currently have it or not).

Here is where it gets interesting: Cross compare your current actual mindset, which you previously articulated in step four, to the desired optimal mindset that you just wrote. It is critical to note whether the two mindsets match or if they differ.

Chapter 23

DIAGRAM 1.1 ASSESSMENT & IDENTIFICATION

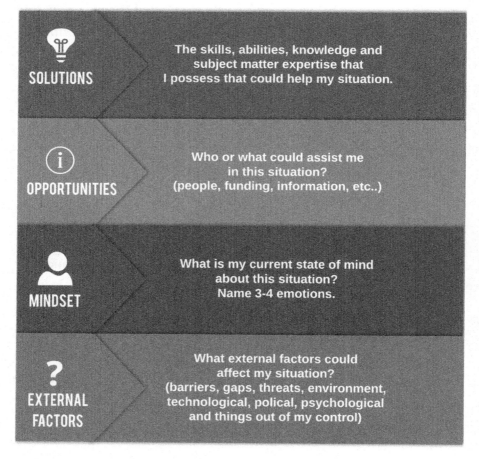

If the two mindsets match, then you are in the perfect position to move forward and succeed. However, if the optimal mindset differs from your actual mindset, then you have a bit of work to do first.

You need to find a way to change your existing perspective about your situation to be able to change your mindset to be a closer match to the desired one. Regardless of your insecurities and your fears, you must push through them all to strive toward a better perspective. The good news is when there is a gap, there is an opportunity and when there is opportunity, breakthrough can happen.

One of the more challenging things you may have to overcome is shifting your perspective on how you see yourself. Self-sabotage and a defeatist attitude are often your most stubborn opponents to bold courage. This is a task like no other in that this is where the rubber hits the proverbial road and you must use bold courage to overcome that negative talk in your head. You cannot succumb to inner messages like "I've tried everything," "I'm a failure," or "It's too broken to be fixed."

Your perspective must prepare you to have a growth mindset where you believe in your own power and ability to achieve and own your awesome no matter the task at hand or how many times you have tried it before.

> Self-sabotage and a defeatist attitude are often your most stubborn opponents to bold courage.

You need fundamentally at least two beliefs: Number one is that the future can be better than the present, and number two is that you have the power to make it so.

If you start holding yourself accountable to these two beliefs you will shift your mindset and create more positive thoughts. All you need is a little belief to get started. As you develop a positive perspective towards your situation, your mindset will also shift to a more positive frame of mind as well.

From my experience and research, here is a brief list of some of the larger common themes that people battle to work through.

> You need fundamentally at least two beliefs: Number one is that the future can be better than the present, and number two is that you have the power to make it so.

- » Bold courage to be open to possibilities
- » Bold courage to be honest with ourselves and others
- » Bold courage to have hope and belief in a better outcome
- » Bold courage to walk through fear
- » Bold courage to be vulnerable
- » Bold courage to have grace with ourselves
- » Bold courage to speak the words: "I can do it," "I am worthy of it," "It is happening for me."
- » Bold courage to ask for help as needed
- » Bold courage to face the future with excitement
- » Bold courage to accept and welcome that you are worthy of greatness
- » Bold courage to accept disappointment without any loss of enthusiasm
- » Bold courage to show respect for yourself
- » Bold courage to recognize the wins and celebrate the effort

There are many more examples that could be added to this list and just because you don't see something there that you are battling with, that doesn't mean it isn't valid. Some of these items are deep rooted and will take time, practice and dedication to overcome.

Shifting your mindset and creating lasting behavioral change doesn't happen overnight. It happens with daily decisions, actions of bold courage and in keeping your commitment to owning your awesome every day.

Once you are able to ensure your perspective has shifted, which in turn will shift your mindset, you are in the perfect position to move forward in the process to advance to own your awesome. Sometimes you may struggle more than others with your perspective and mindset and not be able to reach the optimal mindset. But if you can find at least a little belief, you should move forward with action.

Bold courage is anchored in the idea of taking action despite fear. This is why putting the AWE back into awesome is so important. Shifting your perspective to ensure it is aligned with the right mindset is a crucial part of the process to conquering your commitments in a successful and timely way.

It is only then, through the successful completion of those planned commitments, that you will reach your intended outcome and arrive at owning that moment of awesome you are working toward.

Make no mistake about it. It will feel great when you conquer something! Take time to celebrate and be grateful as you recognize the opportunity you have before you to make positive change for yourself. Congratulations on recognizing the opportunity you have to make positive change for yourself.

The more you are consistent, aligned and capable of implementing a repeatable approach to how you communicate with yourself, the more you will realize success.

The process of using the Success Tracker System is one that should be used throughout your journey and with each outcome that you wish to achieve. At first, the process may seem a little time consuming, but within a short time and a little practice it will become like second nature to you. It won't take you long to run a scenario through it.

Smaller problems that you choose to solve will take less time and thought. Larger and more complex issues naturally will take longer to thoroughly move through the steps of the process. Both scenarios are dependent on you individually, your commitment and your speed of pursuit to achieve success in your intended outcomes.

The Success Tracker System can be applied in life and in work with individuals and with teams. It is a trusted process to define, plan and measure success. With this process you will build capacity and stay actively engaged on the journey to owning your awesome.

PART 6

PUTTING IT ALL TOGETHER

CHAPTER 24

LET FAITH BE YOUR SHELTER

Courage is something you have within you. At times in your life courage may lay dormant, leaving you feeling lost and uncertain. It is at that point when you need to summon your courage to the forefront the most. Typically when you think of using bold courage it is usually related to some crisis, tragedy or calamity when someone has sprung to action and become a hero. While that is true, there is also another way to think of bold courage and that is through the eyes of faith. Having faith in what we cannot see and trusting in the process is part of owning your awesome.

When I was in church as a young child, I learned from my Sunday school teacher about what it means to have faith. She shared a scripture where it spoke about having faith, even if it is as small as a mustard seed. That little bit of faith could move mountains and make a difference. I remember holding that small mustard seed in my hand thinking that faith must be very powerful to be able to make such a difference even in that small state. I now realize that faith, no matter how big or small, has been the only shelter I have been able to depend on for my entire life.

Faith is about the willingness to be vulnerable and trust in the process, despite risking disappointment. You know without a doubt that something has to shift and you are ready and willing to make a change or an impact in a bigger and bolder way.

A little over a decade ago, I was invited to join an international mission team travelling to Balyckchy, Kyrgyzstan which is located in central Asia bordered by Kazakhstan to the north, Uzbekistan to the west, Tajikistan to the southwest and China to the east. I had never heard of that country before and my only reference was to its approximation to Afghanistan and the chaos and fear that were taking place in that country.

For some reason I felt compelled to join the team even though there was an element of risk in travelling to that area of the world. As well, I would be leaving my youngest son (who was only two at the time) behind. He would be safe and I would only be away for few weeks, but I had never ventured away from him before and it was weighing on my mind.

> Faith is about the willingness to be vulnerable and trust in the process, despite risking disappointment.

Faith calls us to take big steps out of our comfort zone at times and this was the time for me. I was worried and excited all at the same time, but despite being nervous about going, I believed it was an incredible opportunity and I should go. Ten months after I made the decision to go, I left home to travel across the world to this unknown country with a team of like-minded caring and passionate professionals who possessed a variety of skills, abilities and expertise and all wanted to make a difference for others. While there, our team was to provide a variety of training supports and construction related improvements to a city of about 40,000 people. My job was to develop a substantial training program for hundreds of women on various themes related to leadership and personal development.

Upon landing in the country, we immediately felt a feeling of insecurity and had no choice but to trust and depend upon our interpreter to guide us through customs and make a smooth entry into the country. My first day there started off with a test to my faith. My luggage was lost so I had nothing of my own in this foreign country. I had to ask our male Russian interpreter to help me barter for underwear and other personal items for myself.

I laugh now when I tell the story and realize it really wasn't the worst thing that could have happened, but at the time it was embarrassing. I certainly held faith at the time that everyone else around me would be unable to understand what my interpreter was asking and pointing to me about.

After a five-hour drive from the airport we arrived in Balykchy, which was surrounded by Issyk-Kul Lake, a pristine glacier lake and incidentally the tenth largest in the world. It is tucked into the Tien Shan Mountains, the same mountain range that renowned terrorist Osama Bin Laden was hiding in at the time.

The fact that we could have come face to face with one of the world's most wanted terrorists who was responsible for thousands of innocent people's deaths wasn't one we took lightly. We all felt a level of vulnerability and insecurity and a feeling of being exposed in a completely foreign country and culture. The threat was real.

When we arrived in Balykchy one view that greeted us was the peaceful and breathtaking sight of the pristine lake. But when we literally turned around and looked at the cityscape view it was anything but beautiful. It was showing the effects of devastation from years of political unrest and ethnic clashes. The city was in ruins and crumbling. Walking through the streets, it was easy to see the toll that poverty had taken on the citizens. The streets were lined with abandoned buildings, broken down vehicles, open sewer drains and starving animals rummaging for scraps. The city was crippled by an unemployment rate of over 80 percent.

Sadly, at the time, Krygystan also had one of the highest rates of orphaned and abandoned children in the world. My heart broke at the sight of all the innocent children who were lost with no families in sight.

I remember thinking as I walked the broken up streets that one of the biggest lessons of life that anyone can learn is about perspective. I know I spoke about it earlier but I continue to think about it a lot and share the importance with my clients.

As I turned from one view to the other, (the pristine lake and the crumbling city) the sheer magnitude of the contrast of the views reminded me of life. One view was crumbling and devastated and the other was beautiful beyond measure. In life we all have areas of devastation and also areas of beauty and sometimes they border each other. When we go through difficult times in our life and have upsetting experiences we often don't understand why and that can be crippling.

When we are experiencing difficult circumstances we often don't see any beauty at all. We feel pain, hopelessness and are most often frustrated and sometimes even angry asking ourselves, "why me?" The only way to get through those trying times is faith. Faith that things will get better and somehow the struggle will all be worth it. Sometimes those situations end up taking us somewhere beautiful and it's easy to see the purpose and other times we never know why we had to endure the struggle, leaving us feeling hopeless and frustrated.

There is something to be said for learning resiliency in life. Resiliency is the ability to overcome any challenge, be it personal or professional, and bounce back stronger and wiser. It's the ability to figuratively fall off a cliff and land softly on your feet with more wisdom and ability that you had before. Resiliency is an important quality since it is what we call upon when life gets tough and we are faced with the inevitable difficulties that have the potential to tear us down.

Unfortunately, the only way to truly learn this trait is to come face to face against obstacles and it is our job to find ways of working through them. The challenges in life may seem unbearable to navigate at the time, but once you are through them you can often see the beauty of the journey on the other side.

Chapter 24

We hear many stories of the underdog and know that despite all odds those people prevail and make it through. They do that by holding onto their faith and the belief that all will be okay. Faith is not only their constant shelter, but is the driver of their hope for the future. Without faith, they are not half as strong as they could be. Lack of faith causes doubts, insecurities, feelings of desperation and fear. By keeping faith in the process of your journey you can conquer anything.

THE HEIGHT OF FAITH

In my journey through the decrepit city I met a woman who reminded me that hope can be restored by having faith. She was a kind 70-year-old woman whose weathered face told a multitude of stories about her challenging life. She was selling sunflower seeds at the side of the road for the equivalent of five United States cents per cup. The woman was literally by a deserted road waiting patiently for her next customer. As I approached her, I looked around me and I was the only one in sight.

As I neared her, her face lit up with joy and pride in her business offering and her desire to serve me. In that moment I did not see desperation or sadness. Instead I saw faith and peace in this woman. She proudly filled a paper cup with sunflower seeds for me and I made my best attempt to communicate with her. In our own broken language exchange, she explained that she was employed in a nearby factory for almost forty years. When the factory closed two years before, she was 68 years old, and she needed to do something to provide for herself, so she decided to start a business. She was proud of her accomplishment and what might have seemed like a silly idea to more advanced nations, was momentous in the life of this woman.

In that country, many women dreamed of owning a business and when they did dream, it was of owning a sunflower seed stand like her. She was considered an inspiration and someone that other women aspired to become. In circumstances that were financially disastrous for the woman, she had faith in her journey and found a way to believe that she could turn it around despite her age, the loss of her job and the economic ruin of her city. She had everything against her starting with her age, economic crisis in her country, corruption, and government upheaval, yet she held faith that she could create a living to sustain her needs. This average, unassuming woman reminded me of the importance of faith in my own journey. Walking away from her stand I pondered about her ability to have faith and the difference it had made in her outcome.

I was so touched by the woman, I thought about her later that day again and admired her ability to achieve her outcome through her challenging times. Her challenges were not like the average North American, who has a meltdown when their cell phone service is out of range. She was struggling for her very survival on a desolate street, having faith that someone would pass by to purchase her seeds so she could afford to eat that day.

I started thinking about my own life and situation and how my own perceptions, resiliency and faith had carried me through some tough times as well. There is one piece of advice when it comes to faith and resilience I will share that I was reminded of that day. Although many situations are not within our control, if we adapt in some way to meet the challenge of the situation and have faith that it will all come together in our favor, it most likely will. It is those people who can adapt to change the fastest are the ones that not only survive, but thrive. By allowing faith to be our shelter, we can get through and adapt to anything. Faith is powerful and my experience with this woman was a real life example of the best of thriving in the midst of adversity and change.

My perspective about my mission trip had been slightly cloaked by worry and fear of the unknown and through my reminder that day, I was quickly able to shift my perspective to something more hopeful. This simple shift of my attitude changed my mindset and to that end allowed me to experience something incredible. Adjusting your perspective is key to anchoring the right mindset for affecting positive change and even in the unknown, faith can and will carry you through if you allow it.

My weeks in Kyrgystan, following that chance meeting with the street vendor, were weeks met with several challenging moments. There were times of feeling uncertain, uncomfortable, and even unsafe. During those times I let my faith carry me, and because of that I had peace that in the end everything would be okay. While there, I found many opportunities to feel blessed and be grateful for. The mindset that I embraced resulted in great impact for those I was there to help, and also left a lasting impression on many, myself included.

CHOOSE BOLD COURAGE

Choose bold courage. Have faith in bold courage. Let faith and bold courage be your gateway to a more fulfilled and satisfied life. Bold courage is the best way to honor your soul, respect your strengths, and learn how to step up and step into owning your awesome. You know it won't always be perfect, since life doesn't work that way. But in the end you know that it will be worth it.

At times life will be downright messy and at other times exhilarating, but the journey as a whole is yours and yours alone to live and thrive within should you choose to. Hold faith in the process and in the outcome.

The Success Tracker System gives you a concrete process to use in the quest to own your awesome. The process builds motivation to live with excellence as you accomplish and realize results from your efforts. Bold courage is one of the greatest outcomes of faith. To me, they go hand in hand. Learn to trust in the unknown and be willing to step forward and risk vulnerability in exchange for an opportunity to live fully and passionately.

Owning your awesome changes everything. As you position yourself with the idea of greatness in your life, everything will change. When you answer that call of 'awesome' into your life, even one small courageous step each day starts to make a difference. You will start to see more and more positive outcomes around you and the others you inspire along the way.

Nearly a decade after being reminded of the power of faith, I was reminded again of this same advice in another unlikely place. I went to see the movie *The Second Best Exotic Marigold Hotel* one evening and I thought one of the most poignant lines was when Sonny repeatedly said: "Everything will be all right in the end...if it's not all right, then it's not the end."

Let faith and bold courage carry you.

CPSIA information can be obtained
at www.ICGtesting.com
Printed in the USA
LVOW04s1036061016
507409LV00001B/1/P